CONGRESSIONAL POLICIES, PRACTICES AND PROCEDURES

THE BASIS AND LIMITATIONS OF CONGRESSIONAL POWER

CONGRESSIONAL POLICIES, PRACTICES AND PROCEDURES

Additional books in this series can be found on Nova's website under the Series tab.

Additional E-books in this series can be found on Nova's website under the E-books tab.

CONGRESSIONAL POLICIES, PRACTICES AND PROCEDURES

THE BASIS AND LIMITATIONS OF CONGRESSIONAL POWER

ARLENE P. BOEHM
AND
MICHAEL D. ANGELLO
EDITORS

Nova Science Publishers, Inc.
New York

For permission to use material from this book please contact us:
Telephone 631-231-7269; Fax 631-231-8175
Web Site: http://www.novapublishers.com

Library of Congress Cataloging-in-Publication Data

The basis and limitations of congressional power / editors, Arlene P. Boehm and Michael D. Angello.
p. cm.
CRS report for Congress.
Includes index.
ISBN 978-1-61324-160-8 (softcover)
1. Legislative power--United States. 2. Interstate commerce--Law and legislation--United States. I. Boehm, Arlene P. II. Angello, Michael D.
KF4930.A25 2011
342.73'052--dc22

2011008484

Published by Nova Science Publishers, Inc. † New York

CONTENTS

PREFACE

The lines of authority between states and the federal government are, to a significant extent, defined by the United States Constitution and relevant case law. In recent years, however, the Supreme Court has decided a number of cases that would seem to reevaluate this historical relationship. This new book discusses the basis and limits of state and federal legislative power, focusing on a number of these "federalism" cases, state sovereignty and the Constitution.

Chapter 1- The lines of authority between states and the federal government are, to a significant extent, defined by the United States Constitution and relevant case law. In recent years, however, the Supreme Court has decided a number of cases that would seem to reevaluate this historical relationship. This report discusses state and federal legislative power generally, focusing on a number of these “federalism” cases. The report does not, however, address the larger policy issue of when it is appropriate—as opposed to constitutionally permissible—to exercise federal powers.

Chapter 2- The Commerce Clause of the United States Constitution provides that the Congress shall have the power to regulate interstate and foreign commerce. The plain meaning of this language might indicate a limited power to regulate commercial trade between persons in one state and persons outside of that state. However, the Commerce Clause has never been construed quite so narrowly. Rather, the clause, along with the economy of the United States, has grown and become more complex. In addition, when Congress began to address national social problems, the Commerce Clause was often cited as the constitutional basis for such legislation. As a result, the Commerce Clause has become the constitutional basis for a significant portion of the laws passed by the Congress over the last fifty years, and it currently represents one of the broadest bases for the exercise of congressional powers. The reliance of the Congress on the Commerce Clause, however, has been controversial, as was the case with the passage of the Patient Protection and Affordable Care Act (PPACA, P.L. 111-148).

The Basis and Limitations of Congressional... ISBN: 978-1-61324-160-8
Editors: A. P. Boehm, M. D. Angello

Chapter 1

FEDERALISM, STATE SOVEREIGNTY, AND THE CONSTITUTION: BASIS AND LIMITS OF CONGRESSIONAL POWER*

Kenneth R. Thomas

SUMMARY

The lines of authority between states and the federal government are, to a significant extent, defined by the United States Constitution and relevant case law. In recent years, however, the Supreme Court has decided a number of cases that would seem to reevaluate this historical relationship. This report discusses state and federal legislative power generally, focusing on a number of these "federalism" cases. The report does not, however, address the larger policy issue of when it is appropriate—as opposed to constitutionally permissible—to exercise federal powers.

The U.S. Constitution provides that Congress shall have the power to regulate commerce with foreign nations and among the various states. This power has been cited as the constitutional basis for a significant portion of the laws passed by Congress over the last 50 years, and, in conjunction with the Necessary and Proper Clause, it currently represents one of the broadest bases for the exercise of congressional powers. In *United States v. Lopez* and subsequent cases, however, the Supreme Court did bring into question the

* This is an edited, reformatted and augmented version of a **Congressional Research Services** publication, dated July 12, 2010.

extent to which Congress can rely on the Commerce Clause as a basis for federal jurisdiction.

Another significant source of congressional power is the Fourteenth Amendment, specifically the Equal Protection and Due Process Clauses. Section 5 of that amendment provides that Congress has the power to enforce its provisions. In the case of *Flores v. City of Boerne*, however, the Court imposed limits on this power, requiring that there must be a "congruence and proportionality" between the injury to be remedied and the law adopted to that end.

The Tenth Amendment provides that "powers not delegated to the United States by the Constitution, nor prohibited by it to the States, are reserved to the States respectively, or to the people." While this language would appear to represent one of the most clear examples of a federalist principle in the Constitution, it has not had a significant impact in limiting federal powers. However, in *New York v. United States* and *Printz v. United States*, the Court did find that, under the Tenth Amendment, Congress cannot "commandeer" either the legislative process of a state or the services of state executive branch officials.

The Eleventh Amendment provides that "[t]he Judicial power of the United States shall not be construed to extend to any suit in law or equity, commenced or prosecuted against one of the United States by Citizens of another State." Although this text is limited to preventing citizens from bringing diversity cases against states in federal courts, the Supreme Court has expanded the concept of state sovereign immunity further to prohibit citizens generally from bringing suits against states under federal law generally. There are exceptions to this limitation, however, and Congress also has a limited ability to abrogate such state immunity.

Finally, Congress has the power under the Spending Clause to require states to undertake certain activities as a condition of receiving federal monies. Such conditions, however, must be related to the underlying grant, and the financial consequences of non-compliance cannot be coercive.

INTRODUCTION

The lines of authority between states and the federal government are, to a significant extent, defined by the United States Constitution and relevant case law. In recent years, however, the Supreme Court has decided a number of cases that would seem to be a reevaluation of this historical relationship. This report discusses state and federal legislative power generally and focuses on a number of these "federalism" cases. The report discusses state and federal legislative power generally, and focuses on a number of these "federalism" cases.[1] Issues addressed include congressional power under the Commerce Clause and the Fourteenth

Amendment; limits on congressional powers, such as the Tenth Amendment; and state sovereign immunity under the Eleventh Amendment. The report does not, however, address the much larger federalism issue of when it is appropriate—as opposed to constitutionally permissible—for federal powers to be exercised.

POWERS OF THE STATES

States may generally legislate on all matters within their territorial jurisdiction. This "police power" does not arise from the Constitution, but is an inherent attribute of the states' territorial sovereignty. The Constitution does, however, provide certain specific limitations on that power. For instance, a state is relatively limited in its authority regarding the regulation of foreign imports and exports[2] or the conduct of foreign affairs.[3] Further, states must respect the decisions of courts of other states,[4] and are limited in their ability to vary their territory without congressional permission.[5] In addition, the Supreme Court has found that states are limited in their ability to burden interstate commerce.[6]

POWERS OF THE FEDERAL GOVERNMENT

The powers of the federal government, while limited to those enumerated in the Constitution,[7] have been interpreted broadly, so as to create a large potential overlap with state authority. For instance, Article I, § 8, cl. 18 provides that "[t]he Congress shall have power "...To make all laws which shall be necessary and proper for carrying into Execution the foregoing Powers, and all other Powers vested by this Constitution in the Government of the United States, or in any Department or Officer thereof." Early in the history of the Constitution, the Supreme Court found that this clause enlarges rather than narrows the powers of Congress.[8]

Congress has broad financial powers, including the power to tax and spend in order to pay debts and provide for the common defense and general welfare of the United States.[9] Congress also has the power to borrow money and to appropriate money from the United States Treasury.[10] The purposes for which Congress may tax and spend are very broad and are not limited by the scope of other enumerated powers under which Congress may regulate.[11] On the other hand, Congress has no power to regulate "for the general welfare," but may only tax and spend for that purpose.

Congress also has broad authority over the commercial interests of the nation, including the power to regulate commerce,[12] to establish bankruptcy laws,[13] to coin money,[14] to punish counterfeiters,[15] to establish post offices and post roads,[16] and to grant patents and copyrights.[17] The Commerce Clause, discussed in more detail below, is one of the most far-reaching grants of power to Congress. Regulation of interstate commerce covers all movement of people and things across state lines, including communication and transportation.

Congress has broad powers over citizenship, including the power to define the circumstances under which immigrants may become citizens,[18] and to protect the rights of those persons who have citizenship. The Fourteenth Amendment gives Congress the power to enforce the guarantees of the Fourteenth Amendment, including the right to due process and equal protection.[19] This power extends specifically to the power of Congress to protect the rights of citizens who are at least 18[20] to vote regardless of race, color, previous condition of servitude,[21] or sex.[22] Congress may also regulate the time, place, and manner of federal elections,[23] and judge the result of such elections.[24] Congress also has a number of other powers relating to elections and appointments.[25]

Congress has the power and authority to purchase and administer property, and has power over those jurisdictions that are not controlled by states, such as the District of Columbia and the territories.[26] Congress is limited by the Fifth Amendment, however, in the taking of private property without compensation.[27] Congress has numerous powers related to war and the protection of the United States and its sovereign interests.[28]

THE COMMERCE CLAUSE

As noted above, the U.S. Constitution provides that Congress shall have the power to regulate commerce with foreign nations and among the various states.[29] This power has been cited as the constitutional basis for a significant portion of the laws passed by Congress over the last 50 years, and it currently represents one of the broadest bases for the exercise of congressional powers. In *United States v. Lopez*,[30] however, the Supreme Court brought into question the extent to which Congress can rely on the Commerce Clause as a basis for federal jurisdiction.

Under the Gun-Free School Zones Act of 1990, Congress made it a federal offense for "any individual knowingly to possess a firearm at a place that the individual knows, or has reasonable cause to believe, is a school zone."[31] In *Lopez*, the Court held that, because the act neither regulated a commercial activity nor contained a requirement that the possession was connected to interstate commerce, the act exceeded the authority of Congress under the Commerce Clause. Although the Court did not explicitly overrule any previous rulings upholding federal statutes passed under the authority of the Commerce Clause, the decision would appear to suggest new limits to Congress's legislative authority.

The scope and extent of the Commerce Clause does not appear to have been of particular concern to the framers of the Constitution.[32] There are indications that the founding fathers considered the federal regulation of commerce to be an important power of the new Constitution primarily as a means of facilitating trade and of raising revenue.[33] While the Anti-Federalists argued that the new Constitution gave too much power to the federal government, they apparently did not raise significant objections to the granting of power to regulate interstate commerce.[34]

The Supreme Court, however, developed an expansive view of the Commerce Clause relatively early in the history of judicial review. For instance, Chief Justice Marshall wrote in 1824 that "the power over commerce ... is vested in Congress as absolutely as it would be in a single government ..." and that "the influence which their constituents possess at elections, are ... the sole restraints" on this power.[35] However, the issue in most of the early Supreme Court Commerce Clause cases dealt not with the limits of congressional authority, but on the implied limitation of the Commerce Clause on a state's ability to regulate commerce.[36]

It has been suggested that the Commerce Clause should be restricted to the regulation of "selling, buying, bartering and transporting."[37] In fact, much of the federal legislation approved of by the Supreme Court early in the 20th century did relate to issues such as the regulation of lottery tickets,[38] the transporting of adulterated food,[39] and the interstate transportation of prostitutes.[40] Moreover, during the early 1900s, the Supreme Court struck down a series of federal statutes that attempted to extend commerce regulation to activities such as "production," "manufacturing,"[41] and "mining."[42]

Starting in 1937, however, with the decision in *NLRB v. Jones & Laughlin Steel Corporation*,[43] the Supreme Court held that Congress has the ability to protect interstate commerce from burdens and obstructions that "affect" commerce transactions. In the *NLRB* case, the court upheld the National Labor Relations Act, finding that by controlling industrial labor strife, Congress was preventing burdens from being placed on interstate commerce.[44] Thus, the Court rejected previous distinctions between the economic activities (such as manufacturing) that led up to interstate economic transactions, and the interstate transactions themselves. By allowing Congress to regulate activities that were in the "stream" of commerce, the Court also set the stage for the regulation of a variety of other activities that "affect" commerce.

Subsequent Court decisions found that Congress had considerable discretion in determining which activities "affect" interstate commerce, as long as the legislation was "reasonably" related to achieving its goals of regulating interstate commerce.[45] Thus the Court found that in some cases, events of purely local commerce (such as local working conditions) might, because of market forces, negatively affect the regulation of interstate commerce, and thus would be susceptible to regulation.[46] The Court has also held that an activity which in itself does not affect interstate commerce could be regulated if all such activities taken in the aggregate did affect interstate commerce.[47] Under the reasoning of these cases, the Court has upheld many diverse laws, including laws regulating production of wheat on farms,[48] racial discrimination by businesses,[49] and loan-sharking.[50]

The *Lopez* case was significant in that it is the first time since 1937 that the Supreme Court struck down a federal statute purely based on a finding that Congress had exceeded its powers under the Commerce Clause.[51] In doing so, the Court revisited its prior cases, sorted the commerce power into three categories, and asserted that Congress could not go beyond these three categories: (1) regulation of channels of commerce, (2) regulation of instrumentalities of commerce, and (3) regulation of economic activities that "affect" commerce.[52]

Within the third category of activities that "affect commerce," the Court determined that the power to regulate commerce applies to intrastate activities only when they "substantially" affect commerce.[53] Still, the Court in *Lopez* spoke approvingly of earlier cases upholding laws that regulated intrastate credit transactions, restaurants utilizing interstate supplies, and hotels catering to interstate guests. The Court also recognized that while some intrastate activities may by themselves have a trivial effect on commerce, regulation of these activities may be constitutional if their regulation is an essential part of a larger economic regulatory scheme. Thus, the Court even approved what has been perceived as one of its most expansive rulings, *Wickard v. Filburn*, which allowed the regulation of the production and consumption of wheat for home consumption.[54]

The Court in *Lopez* found, however, that the Gun-Free School Zones Act fell into none of the three categories set out above. It held that it is not a regulation of channels of commerce, nor does it protect an instrumentality of commerce. Finally, its effect on interstate commerce was found to be too removed to be "substantial." The Court noted that the regulated activity, possessing guns in school, neither by itself nor in the aggregate affected commercial transactions.[55] Further, the statute contained no requirement that interstate commerce be affected, such as that the gun had been previously transported in interstate commerce.[56] Nor was the criminalization of possession of a gun near a school part of a larger regulatory scheme that did regulate commerce.[57] Finally, the Court indicated that criminal law enforcement is an area of law traditionally reserved to the states.[58] Consequently, the Court found that Congress did not have the authority to pass the Gun-Free School Zone Act.

It should be noted that the *Lopez* Court purported to be limiting, but not overruling, prior case law that had supported an expansive interpretation of the commerce clause. Consequently, most existing federal laws, which have traditionally been drafted to be consistent with this case law,[59] would survive constitutional scrutiny even under *Lopez.* However, in at least one significant case, Congress passed a law, the Violence Against Women Act, that seemed to invoke the same concerns that the Court found in *Lopez.* Consequently, the relevant portion of that act was struck down in *United States v. Morrison.*[60]

In *Morrison*, the Court evaluated whether 42 U.S.C. § 13981, which provides a federal private right of action for victims of gender-motivated violence, was within the power of Congress to enact under the Commerce Clause. In *Morrison*, the victim of an alleged rape brought suit against the alleged rapist, arguing that this portion of the act was sustainable because it addressed activities that substantially affect interstate commerce.[61] The Court, however, noted that unlike traditional statutes based on the commerce clause, the activity in question had nothing to do with commerce or an economic enterprise. This point had been made previously in *Lopez*, and here the Court reaffirmed the holding that in order to fall under the acceptable category of laws that "substantially affect commerce," the underlying activity itself must generally be economic or commercial.[62] As gender-motivated violence does not inherently relate to an economic activity, the Court held that it was beyond the authority of Congress to regulate.

In the case of *Gonzales v. Raich*,[63] the Court evaluated an "as applied" challenge to the Controlled Substances Act as regards obtaining, manufacturing, or possessing marijuana for medical purposes. The case was brought by two seriously ill residents of California who used marijuana in compliance with the California Compassionate Use Act of 1996.[64] The challenge was based on the argument that the narrow class of activity being engaged in—the intrastate, noncommercial cultivation and possession of cannabis for personal medical purposes as recommended by a patient's physician pursuant to valid California state law—did not have a substantial impact on commerce, and thus could not be regulated under the Commerce Clause.[65]

In upholding the application of the Controlled Substances Act in the *Raich* case, the Court relied on its decision in *Wickard v. Filburn*,[66] which held that "even if appellee's activity be local and though it may not be regarded as commerce, it may still, whatever its nature, be reached by Congress if it exerts a substantial economic effect on interstate commerce."[67] The *Wickard* case upheld the application of the Agricultural Adjustment Act of 1938,[68] which was designed to control prices by regulating the volume of wheat moving in interstate commerce. The Court in *Wickard* held that Congress could regulate not only the wheat sold into commerce, but also wheat retained for consumption on a farm.[69] The Court did so on the theory that the while the impact of wheat consumed on the farm on interstate commerce might be trivial, it was significant when combined with wheat from other farmers similarly situated.[70]

Based on *Wickard*, the Court in *Raich* held that Congress could consider the aggregate effect that allowing the production and consumption of marijuana for medical purposes would have on the illegal market for marijuana.[71] Of even greater concern was that diversion of marijuana grown for medicinal purposes for other uses would frustrate the federal interest in eliminating commercial transactions in the interstate market.[72] In both cases, the Court found that the regulation was within Congress's commerce power because Congress had a rational basis to determine that production of a commodity meant for home consumption, be it wheat or marijuana, could have a substantial effect on supply and demand. In addition, because exempting the use of medical marijuana could undercut enforcement of the Controlled Substances Act, the Court found that the application in this case was within Congress's authority to "make all Laws which shall be necessary and proper" to effectuate its powers.

THE NECESSARY AND PROPER CLAUSE

The Constitution provides Congress not only enumerated powers, but also the ability to pass laws to make such powers effective. While such a power might have been implied of necessity even without an explicit textual basis in the Constitution, the Founding Fathers specifically included congressional authority to "make all Laws which shall be necessary and proper"[73] to effectuate its powers. Although the extension of congressional power under this clause is not an independent basis for legislation, the provision has been integral to a broad interpretation of other congressional powers. For instance, as discussed below, the expansive nature of modern Commerce Clause doctrine may actually be a reflection of Necessary and Proper Clause jurisprudence.

Sometimes, the Court's reliance on the Necessary and Proper Clause in a particular case is only briefly noted, or may even exist *sub silentio*. For instance, the majority opinion in the case of *Gonzales v. Raich* (discussed above) emphasized that, in evaluating the scope of Congress's authority under the Commerce Clause to regulate medicinal marijuana, the Court need only find that Congress had a "rational basis" to find a link between the legislation and the Commerce Clause. The Court then went on to note that in such cases "Congress was acting well within its authority to 'make all Laws which shall be necessary and proper' to 'regulate Commerce ... among the several States.'"[74] This language then served to allow the Court to approve the restriction of medical marijuana as one component of a larger economic regulatory scheme.

This passing reference to the Necessary and Proper Clause may obscure its historical significance to Commerce Clause litigation. Writing in concurrence in *Raich*, Justice Scalia argued that it is more accurate to characterize the expansive "substantial effects" prong of Commerce Clause analysis as predominantly based on the Necessary and Proper Clause. He noted that the current description of the "substantial effects" prong is misleading because, unlike the channels, instrumentalities, and agents of interstate commerce, activities that substantially affect interstate commerce are not themselves part of interstate commerce, and thus the power to regulate them cannot come from the Commerce Clause alone. Rather, "as this Court has acknowledged ...

Congress's regulatory authority over intrastate activities that are not themselves part of interstate commerce (including activities that have a substantial effect on interstate commerce) derives from the Necessary and Proper Clause."[75] In fact, Justice Scalia argues that, in some cases, the Necessary and Proper Clause can go beyond existing doctrines of the Commerce Clause, to regulate even those intrastate activities that do not themselves substantially affect interstate commerce.

Another area where the Court has provided a similarly broad interpretation of an Article I congressional power based on the Necessary and Proper Clause is the Spending Clause.[76] In *Sabri v. United States*,[77] the Court considered whether the federal government could punish the bribery of state, local, and tribal officials if the governmental entities that employed them received at least $10,000 in federal funds. The defendant, who was convicted of attempting to bribe a city councilman to facilitate the building of a hotel and retail structure in Minneapolis, argued that the statute in question had no federal nexus. The Court rejected this argument, holding that Congress's authority under the Spending Clause, when supplemented by the Necessary and Proper Clause, allowed Congress to ensure that federal dollars not be diverted or undermined by corruption. The Court held that it was not important if the federal funds received by the governmental entity in question were not directly involved in a particular scheme, because "money is fungible, bribed officials are untrustworthy stewards of federal funds, and corrupt contractors do not deliver dollar-for-dollar value."[78]

An even more expansive interpretation of the Necessary and Proper Clause, in this case as applied to the entire federal criminal penal system (which derives from a variety of congressional powers), is found in the Court's opinion in *United States v. Comstock.*[79] In *Comstock,* the Court evaluated a federal statute which allowed for the civil commitment of a federal prisoner past the term of his or her imprisonment, if that prisoner would have serious difficultly in refraining from sexually violent conduct or child molestation. The statute contained no requirement that the threatened future conduct would fall under federal jurisdiction, raising the question of what constitutional basis could be cited for the enforcement of the statute.

The majority opinion in *Comstock* upheld the statute after considering five factors: (1) the historic breadth of the Necessary and Proper Clause; (2) the history of federal involvement in this area; (3) the reason for the statute's enactment; (4) the statute's accommodation of state interests; and (5) whether the scope of the statute was too attenuated from Article I powers.[80] The Court noted that the breadth of the power was established by Justice Marshall in the case of *McCulloch v. Maryland,*[81] where the Chief Justice wrote:

> Let the end be legitimate, let it be within the scope of the Constitution, and all means which are appropriate, which are plainly adapted to that end, which are not prohibited, but consist with the letter and spirit of the Constitution, are Constitutional.

Previous federal involvement in the area included not only the civil commitment of defendants who were incompetent to stand trial or who became insane during the course of their imprisonment, but, starting in 1949, the continued confinement of those adjudged incompetent or insane past the end of their prison term.

In upholding the sex offender statute, the Court found that protection of the public and the probability that such prisoners would not be committed by the state represented a rational basis for the passage of such legislation. The Court further found that the state interests were protected by the legislation, as the statute provided for transfer of the committed individuals to state authorities willing to accept them. Finally, the Court found that the statute was not too attenuated from the Article I powers underlying the criminal laws which had been the basis for incarceration, as it related to the responsible administration of the United States prison system.

THE FOURTEENTH AMENDMENT

Another significant source of congressional power is § 5 of the Fourteenth Amendment. The Fourteenth Amendment provides that states shall not deprive citizens of "life, liberty or property" without due process of law nor deprive them of equal protection of the laws. Section 5 provides that Congress has the power to legislate to enforce the amendment.

The Fourteenth Amendment represented a significant shift of power in the nation's federal system. Until the passage of the Fourteenth Amendment, the Constitution was limited to establishing the powers and limitations of the federal government. However, the amendments passed immediately after the Civil War (the Thirteenth,[82] Fourteenth, and Fifteenth[83] Amendments), dramatically altered this regime. Passage of these amendments subjected a state's control over its own citizens to oversight by either the federal judiciary or Congress. The most significant impact of the Fourteenth Amendment has been its implementation by the federal courts, as state legislation came under scrutiny for having violated due process or equal protection. However, Congress has also seen fit to exercise its power under the Fourteenth Amendment to address issues such as voting rights and police brutality.

The scope of Congress's power under § 5 of the Fourteenth Amendment, however, has been in flux over the years. In *Katzenbach v. Morgan*,[84] the Court held that § 5 of the Fourteenth Amendment authorized Congress not just to enforce the provisions of the Fourteenth Amendment as defined by the courts, but to help define its scope. In *Katzenbach*, the Court upheld a portion of the Voting Rights Act of 1965 that barred the application of English literacy requirements to persons who had reached 6th grade in a Puerto Rican school taught in Spanish. In upholding the statute, the Court rejected the argument that Congress's power to legislate under the Fourteenth Amendment was limited to enforcing that which the Supreme Court found to be a violation of that amendment. Rather, the Court held that Congress could enforce the Fourteenth Amendment by "appropriate" legislation consistent with the "letter and spirit of the constitution."

The rationale for this holding appears to be that Congress has the ability to evaluate and address factual situations that it determines may lead to degradation of rights protected under the Fourteenth Amendment. This is true even if a court would not find a constitutional violation to have occurred. In fact, what the Court appeared to have done was to require only that Congress establish a rational basis for why the legislation was necessary to protect a Fourteenth Amendment right.

Subsequent Supreme Court cases, however, have limited the reach of *Katzenbach*. In *Oregon v. Mitchell*,[85] the Court struck down a requirement that the voting age be lowered to 18 for state elections. In prohibiting Congress from dictating the voting age for state elections, a splintered Court appears to have supported Congress's power to pass laws that protect Fourteenth Amendment rights against state intrusions, but rejected the ability of Congress to extend the substantive content of those rights. As 18-year-olds are not a protected class under the Fourteenth Amendment, the Court found that Congress was attempting to create, rather than protect, Fourteenth Amendment rights.

More recently, in the case of *Flores v. City of Boerne*,[86] the Court struck down the Religious Freedom Restoration Act (RFRA) as beyond the authority of Congress under § 5 of the Fourteenth Amendment. For many years prior to the passage of RFRA, a law of general applicability restricting the free exercise of religion, to be consistent with the Freedom of Exercise Clause of the First Amendment, had to be justified by a compelling governmental interest. However, in the 1990 case of *Oregon v. Smith*,[87] the Court had lowered this standard. The *Smith* case involved members of the Native American Church who were denied unemployment benefits when they lost their jobs for having used peyote during a religious ceremony. The *Smith* case held that neutral generally applicable laws may be applied to religious practices even if the law is not supported by a compelling governmental interest. RFRA, in response, was an attempt by Congress to overturn the *Smith* case, and to require a compelling governmental interest when a state applied a generally applied law to religion.

The *City of Boerne* case arose when the City of Boerne denied a church a building permit to expand, because the church was in a designated historical district. The church challenged the zoning decision under RFRA. The Supreme Court reiterated that § 5 of the Fourteenth Amendment gave Congress the power to enforce existing constitutional protections, but found that this did not automatically include the power to pass any legislation to protect these rights. Instead, the Court held that there must be a "congruence and proportionality" between the injury to be remedied and the law adopted to that end. For instance, the Court's decision in *Katzenbach v. Morgan* of allowing the banning of literacy tests was justified based on an extensive history of minorities being denied suffrage in this country. In contrast, the Court found no similar pattern of the use of neutral laws of general applicability disguising religious bigotry and animus against religion. Rather than an attempt to remedy a problem, RFRA was seen by the Court as an attempt by Congress to overturn an unpopular Supreme Court decision. The law focused on no one area of alleged harm to religion, but rather just broadly inhibited state and local regulations of all types. Consequently, the Court found RFRA to be an overbroad response to a relatively nonexistent problem.

The scope of the enforcement power under § 5 of the Fourteenth Amendment also has become important in cases where the Court has found that Congress has overreached its power under other provision of the Constitution, or is limited by some provision thereof. For instance, as discussed in detail below, the Supreme Court has held that the Eleventh Amendment and state sovereign immunity generally prohibit individuals from suing states for damages under federal law.[88] However, the Supreme Court has also held that Congress can abrogate state sovereign immunity under the Fourteenth Amendment.[89] This means that in many cases, litigants suing states will have to find a Fourteenth Amendment basis for federal legislation in order to defeat an Eleventh Amendment defense. For instance, a significant amount of federal legislation is clearly supported by the commerce clause, but it might not be supported under § 5. Recently, the Court decided two cases that illustrate the difficulties of establishing Fourteenth Amendment authority for such legislation.

In *College Savings Bank v. Florida Prepaid Postsecondary Education Expense Board*,[90] the Supreme Court considered an unfair competition suit brought by a New Jersey savings bank against the state of Florida. The New Jersey savings bank had developed a patented program where individuals could use a certificate of deposit contract to save for college. The state of Florida set up a similar program, and the College Savings Bank sued Florida for false and misleading advertising under a provision of the Trademark Act of 1946 (Lanham Act),[91] alleging that Florida had made misleading representations about its own product.

The Court first noted that under *Seminole Tribe of Florida v. Florida*, Article I, powers such as the power to regulate commerce were insufficient to abrogate Eleventh Amendment immunity. Thus, the Court next considered whether the Lanham Act could be characterized as an exercise of Congress's power under § 5 of the Fourteenth Amendment. Although the Fourteenth Amendment provides that no state shall "deprive a person of ... property ... without due process of law," the Court found that the unfair trade in question, which consisted of allegedly inaccurate statements made by the state of Florida about its own saving program, did not infringe on any exclusive property right held by the College Savings Bank. As the Court found that Congress had not established an authority under the Fourteenth Amendment to abrogate the state's immunity, the College Savings Bank could not proceed against the state of Florida for unfair trade practices.

Even if a property interest is established, it would still need to be determined that Congress had the authority to protect that property interest under the Fourteenth Amendment. In *Florida Prepaid Postsecondary Education Expense Board v. College Savings Bank*,[92] the Court, in a decision concerning the same parties as the case discussed above, considered whether the College Savings Bank could sue the state of Florida for patent infringement. Congress had passed a law specifically providing that states could be sued for patent violations,[93] citing three sources of constitutional authority: the Article I Patent Clause,[94] the Article I Interstate Commerce Clause,[95] and § 5 of the Fourteenth Amendment. As the Court had previously precluded abrogation of sovereign immunity through the exercise of Article I powers, the question became whether Congress had the authority to pass patent legislation under § 5 of the Fourteenth Amendment.

Unlike the previous case, the Court found that, under a long line of precedents, patents were considered property rights. However, the Court had to further consider whether the protection of such a property right under § 5 of the Fourteenth Amendment was "appropriate" under its ruling in *City of Boerne*. Consequently, the Court evaluated whether a federal right to enforce patents against states was appropriate remedial or preventive legislation aimed at securing the protections of the Fourteenth Amendment for patent owners. Specifically, the Court sought to evaluate whether unremedied patent infringement by states rose to the level of a Fourteenth Amendment violation that Congress could redress.

The Court noted that Congress had failed to identify a pattern of patent infringement by the states, and that only a handful of patent infringement cases had been brought against states in the last 100 years. The Court also noted that Congress had failed to establish that state remedies for patent infringement were inadequate for citizens to seek compensation for injury. In fact, the state of Florida argued that no constitutionally based violation had occurred, as it had procedures in place that would provide the necessary due process for patent infringement by the state to be challenged. Consequently, the Court found that the exercise of § 5 of the Fourteenth Amendment in this context would be out of proportion to the remedial objective.

The Court engaged in a similar analysis, with like results, in evaluating the application of age discrimination laws to the states. In *Kimel v. Florida Board of Regents*,[96] the Court noted that the Age Discrimination in Employment Act of 1967, while a valid exercise of Congress's commerce power, could not be applied to the states unless Congress also had the power to enact it under § 5 of the Fourteenth Amendment. The *Kimel* Court held, however, that age is not a suspect class, and that the provisions of the ADEA far surpassed the kind of protections that would be afforded such a class under the Fourteenth Amendment. Further, the Court found that an analysis of Congress's ability to legislate prophylactically under section § 5 required an examination of the legislative record to determine whether the remedies provided were proportional and congruent to the problem. A review by the Court of the ADEA legislative record found no evidence of a pattern of state governments discriminating against employees on the basis of age. Consequently, the Court held that a state could not be liable for damages under the ADEA.

Similarly, the application of Title I of the Americans with Disabilities Act (ADA) to states was considered in the case of the *Board of Trustees v. Garrett*,[97] again with similar result. In *Garrett,* the Court evaluated whether two plaintiffs could bring claims for money damages against a state university for failing to make reasonable employment accommodations for their disabilities; one plaintiff was under treatment for cancer, the other for asthma and sleep apnea. Although disability is not a suspect class and thus discrimination is evaluated under a rational basis test, the Court had previously shown a heightened sensitivity to arbitrary discrimination against the disabled.[98]

Further, Congress had made substantial findings regarding the pervasiveness of such discrimination. However, the Supreme Court declined to consider evidence of discrimination by either the private sector or local government, and dismissed the examples that did relate to the states as unlikely to rise to the level of constitutionally "irrational" discrimination. Ultimately, the Court found that no pattern of unconstitutional state discrimination against the disabled had been established, and that the application of the ADA was not a proportionate response to any pattern that might exist.

However, the Court reached a different conclusion in the case of *Nevada Department of Human Resources v. Hibbs*.[99] In the *Hibbs* case, an employee of the Nevada Department of Human Resources had a dispute with the Department regarding how much leave time he had available under the Family and Medical Leave Act of 1993 (FMLA). The FMLA requires employers to provide employees up to 12 weeks of unpaid leave to care for a close relative with a "serious health condition."[100] In *Hibbs*, the Court held that Congress had the power to abrogate a state's Eleventh Amendment immunity under the FMLA, so that a state employee could recover money damages. The Court found that Congress had established significant evidence of a long and extensive history of sex discrimination with respect to the administration of leave benefits by the states, and that history was sufficient to justify the enactment of the legislation under § 5. The standard for demonstrating the constitutionality of a gender-based classification is more difficult to meet than the rational-basis test, such was at issue in *Kimel* and *Garrett*, so it was easier for Congress to show a pattern of state constitutional violations.

Even where the Eleventh Amendment and state sovereign immunity are not at issue, the Court may be asked to consider whether the Fourteenth Amendment establishes a sufficient basis for a federal law that does not appear to have a constitutional basis elsewhere in the Constitution. For instance, in *United States v. Morrison*,[101] discussed previously,[102] the Court found that Congress, in creating a federal private right of action for victims of gender-motivated violence, had exceeded its authority under the Commerce Clause. Consequently, the plaintiff in that case made the alternate argument that the federal private right of action could be sustained under § 5 of the Fourteenth Amendment.

This argument, however, suffered from two major defects. First, the Court has long held that the Fourteenth Amendment provides Congress with the authority to regulate states but not individuals.[103] In *Morrison*, however, the civil case had been brought against the individuals alleged to have engaged in the offense. The plaintiff attempted to avoid this problem by arguing that there is pervasive bias in various state justice systems against victims of gender-motivated violence, and that providing a federal private right of action was an appropriate means to remedy this "state action."

However, the Court rejected this argument, finding that the remedy did not meet the *City of Boerne* test of "congruence and proportionality to the injury to be prevented or remedied and the means adopted to that end."[104] Because the federal private right of action was not aimed at the allegedly discriminatory actions by state officials, but was instead directed against the individual engaging in the violence itself, the Court found that the action could not be supported by reference to the Fourteenth Amendment.[105]

The Court again considered the issue of Congress's power under § 5 of the Fourteenth Amendment in *Tennessee v. Lane.*[106] In the *Lane* case, two paraplegic plaintiffs alleged that the state of Tennessee and several of its counties violated Title II of the ADA, which requires that the disabled be provided access to public services, programs, and activities, by failing to provide physical access to state courts.[107] The Court held that Title II, as applied to this right of access to the courts, was a proper exercise of Congress's authority under § 5 of the Fourteenth Amendment to abrogate states' Eleventh Amendment immunity. Similar to its holdings in the *Garrett* and *Hibbs* cases, the Court found that Congress had established sufficient evidence of the sustained denial of persons with disabilities of access to the courts.[108]

In applying the *Boerne* congruence and proportionality test, the Court in *Lane* distinguished the rights Congress intended to protect in Title II (access to public services, programs, and activities) from the Title I employment rights that had been struck down in *Garrett.* While both Titles I and II were intended to address unequal treatment of the disabled (which is only a constitutional violation when it is irrational), the Court held that Title II was also intended to reach the more rigorously protected rights of the Due Process Clause of the Fourteenth

Amendment, such as the right of access to the courts.[109] The Court stated that the due process rights Congress sought to protect under Title II required a standard of judicial review at least as searching as the sex-based classifications the Court considered in *Hibbs*.[110] The limited nature of Title II as a remedy for the denial of the right of access to courts also informed the Court's holding that the measure is a valid prophylactic remedy.[111]

Congress's authority under § 5 of the Fourteenth Amendment to abrogate states' Eleventh Amendment immunity appears strongest when the focus of the prophylactic measure at issue is conduct that actually violates a constitutional right. In *United States v. Georgia*,[112] a disabled state prison inmate who used a wheelchair for mobility alleged that the state of Georgia violated Title II of the ADA in relation to his conditions of confinement. The Court reiterated its holding in *Lane* that Title II is a constitutional exercise of Congress's Fourteenth Amendment powers. It went on to state that Title II was valid as applied to the plaintiff's cause of action, because he alleged independent violations under § 1 of the Fourteenth Amendment concerning his prison treatment.[113]

THE TENTH AMENDMENT

The Tenth Amendment provides that "powers not delegated to the United States by the Constitution, nor prohibited by it to the States, are reserved to the States respectively, or to the people." While this language would appear to represent one of the most clear examples of a federalist principle in the Constitution, it has not had a significant impact in limiting federal powers. Initially, the Supreme Court interpreted the Tenth Amendment to have substantive content, so that certain "core" state functions would be beyond the authority of the federal government to regulate. Thus, in *National League of Cities v. Usery*,[114] the Court struck down federal wage and price controls on state employees as involving the regulation of core state functions.[115] The Court, however, overruled *National League of Cities* in *Garcia v. San Antonio Metropolitan Transit Authority*.[116] In sum, the Court in *Garcia* seems to have said that most disputes over the effects on state sovereignty of federal commerce power legislation are to be considered political questions, and that the states should look for relief from federal regulation through the political process.[117] This appeared to have ended the Court's attempt to substantively limit federal government regulation of the states.

The Court soon turned, however, to the question of how the Constitution limits the process by which the federal government regulates the states. In *New*

York v. United States,[118] Congress had attempted to regulate in the area of low-level radioactive waste. In a 1985 statute, Congress provided that states must either develop legislation on how to dispose of all low-level radioactive waste generated within the state, or the state would be forced to take title to such waste, which would mean that it became the state's responsibility. The Court found that although Congress had the authority under the Commerce Clause to regulate low-level radioactive waste, it only had the power to regulate the waste directly. Here, Congress had attempted to require the states to perform the regulation, and decreed that the failure to do so would require the state to deal with the financial consequences of owning large quantities of radioactive waste. In effect, Congress sought to "commandeer" the legislative process of the states. In the *New York* case, the Court found that this power was not found in the text or structure of the Constitution, and it was thus a violation of the Tenth Amendment.

A later case presented the question of the extent to which Congress could regulate through a state's executive branch officers. This case, *Printz v. United States*,[119] involved the Brady Handgun Act. The Brady Handgun Act required state and local law-enforcement officers to conduct background checks on prospective handgun purchasers within five business days of an attempted purchase. This portion of the act was challenged under the Tenth Amendment, under the theory that Congress was without authority to "commandeer" state executive branch officials. After a historical study of federal commandeering of state officials, the Court concluded that commandeering of state executive branch officials was, like commandeering of the legislature, outside of Congress's power, and consequently a violation of the Tenth Amendment.

Although the federal government is prohibited from commandeering either the legislature or executive branch of a state, this does not appear to be the case with state judicial branches. The federal judicial system and the state judicial system were not intended to be as separate as the other branches of government, and the Supremacy Clause of the Constitution explicitly provides that state courts must follow federal law, even if it overrides state laws or constitutions.[120] So, there appears to be less of a concern regarding the "commandeering" of state courts.

A key distinction between constitutional "substantive regulation" and unconstitutional "commandeering" appears to be whether or not the federal mandate in question is regulating state activities or whether it is seeking to control the manner in which states regulate private parties.

Thus, for instance, the Court recently held in *Reno v. Condon*[121] that the Driver's Privacy Protection Act of 1994, which regulates the sale of personal information gathered from persons seeking drivers licenses, was substantive regulation, not commandeering. In that case, the Court found that the state was not being directed on how to regulate its citizens, but rather on how to treat information that had been elicited from those citizens. However, because the regulation affected both state governments and private resellers of such information, the Court reserved the question as to whether a law, which only regulated state activities, would be constitutionally suspect.

ELEVENTH AMENDMENT AND STATE SOVEREIGN IMMUNITY

The Eleventh Amendment and state sovereign immunity provide an example of the complicated interaction between the powers of the federal government, the state, and the individual. The basic issue to be addressed here is the extent to which individuals can sue a state under federal law.[122] The answer to this question may vary based on a number of factors, including what law the suit is being brought under, whether the state has taken action to make itself amenable to such law, and what relief is being sought.

The starting point for such a discussion is usually the Eleventh Amendment. The Eleventh Amendment reads, in part, as follows: "The Judicial power of the United States shall not be construed to extend to any suit in law or equity, commenced or prosecuted against one of the United States by Citizens of another State." The actual text of the Amendment appears to be limited to preventing U.S. or foreign citizens from bringing diversity cases against states in federal courts. However, the Supreme Court has expanded the concept of state sovereign immunity to reach much further than the text of the amendment.

The Eleventh Amendment, the first amendment to the Constitution after the adoption of the Bill of Rights, was passed as a response to the case of *Chisholm v. Georgia*.[123] Immediately after the adoption of the Constitution, a number of citizens filed cases in federal court against states. One of these, *Chisholm*, was a diversity suit filed by two citizens of South Carolina against the State of Georgia to recover a Revolutionary War debt. In *Chisholm,* the Supreme Court noted that Article III of the Constitution specifically grants the federal courts diversity jurisdiction over suits "between a State and citizens of another State."[124] Thus, the Court held that this grant of jurisdiction authorized the private citizen of one state to sue another state in federal court without that state's consent.

The states were outraged that such a suit could be brought in federal court, protesting that the drafters of the Constitution had promised the states they would not be sued by their debtors in federal courts. Almost immediately after the decision of the *Chisholm* cases, resolutions were introduced in Congress to overturn it, the end result being the Eleventh Amendment. The amendment ensured that a citizen of one state could not sue another state in federal court—in other words, a citizen could not sue under federal diversity jurisdiction without a state's permission.

However, even after the Eleventh Amendment was passed, a number of cases were filed against states by private citizens, with jurisdiction based on federal question rather than diversity. Under this reasoning, if a citizen of a state sued his or her own state in federal court, the prohibition of the Eleventh Amendment would not apply. Consequently, for a number of years after the passage of the Eleventh Amendment, this type of case was entertained by the federal courts. However, this line of cases was ended by the case of *Hans v. Louisiana*.[125]

In *Hans v. Louisiana*, the Court provided for an interpretation of the Eleventh Amendment that allowed the Court to move beyond the literal text of that amendment. Under the reasoning of the Court, the Eleventh Amendment was not so much an amendment to the original structure of the Constitution as it was an attempt to overturn a specific court decision that had misinterpreted this structure. According to this line of reasoning, the Eleventh Amendment was not an amendment, but a restoration of the original constitutional design.

Ultimately, the issue before the Court in *Hans v. Louisiana* and in subsequent cases was not the Eleventh Amendment, but the issue of state sovereign immunity. State sovereign immunity means that a state must consent to be sued in its own court system. This concept is based on early English law, which provided that the Crown could not be sued in English courts without its consent. The doctrine of sovereign immunity was in effect in the states that were in existence at the time of the drafting of the Constitution. Further, various writings by the founding fathers seemed to support the concept.[126] Thus, the issue before the Court in *Hans* was whether the grant of jurisdiction to federal courts under Article III of the Constitution had abrogated state sovereign immunity. The *Hans* Court found that Article III did not have this effect.

Although the *Hans* Court answered the issue of whether adoption of Article III of the Constitution had waived state sovereign immunity in federal courts, it left a number of questions unanswered. For instance, the question as to whether there are any instances where Congress could, by statute, abrogate a state's sovereign immunity, so that a citizen could sue a state under federal law. In *Seminole Tribe of Florida v. Florida,*[127] the Court seemed to answer that in most cases, such suits would not be accepted. The *Seminole* case involved the Indian Gaming Regulatory Act of 1988, which provided Indian tribes with an opportunity to establish gambling operations. However, to establish such gambling, the Indian tribes had to enter into a compact with the state in which they were located. The states, in turn, were obligated to negotiate with the Indian tribes in good faith, and this requirement was made enforceable in federal court. Thus, the question arose as to whether the tribes could sue the states under the Eleventh Amendment.

The Court in *Seminole* found it important to establish what constitutional authority was being exercised by the passage of the Indian Gaming Law. The Court determined that the power being exercised was the Indian Commerce Clause,[128] which is found in Article I. The Court had found previously in *Pennsylvania v. Union Gas*,[129] that the Commerce Power, as a plenary power, was so broad that of necessity it required the ability to abrogate state sovereign immunity. In *Seminole*, however, the Court overturned *Union Gas*, holding that as the Eleventh Amendment was ratified after the passage of the Constitution and Article I, it was a limitation on Congress's authority to waive a state's sovereign immunity under that Article. The Court did indicate, however, that Congress can abrogate state sovereignty under the Fourteenth Amendment. While the logic behind this distinction is unclear,[130] it means that in many cases, litigants suing states will try to find a Fourteenth Amendment basis for federal legislation to defeat an Eleventh Amendment defense.

A question left unanswered by the *Hans* decision was whether the Eleventh Amendment, which prohibited Congress from abrogating a state's sovereign immunity in federal court, extended to a state's own courts. In *Alden v. Maine*,[131] the Supreme Court found that the same principles of sovereign immunity identified in *Hans* would prevent Congress from authorizing a state to be sued in its own courts without permission. As in *Hans*, the Court acknowledged that the literal text of the Eleventh Amendment does not prohibit such suits, as its language addresses only suits brought in federal courts. Consequently, the Court relied instead on the proposition that sovereign immunity is a "fundamental postulate" of the constitutional design, and is not amenable to congressional abrogation. The same reasoning that prohibited these suits from being brought in federal court, a deference to the "respect and dignity" of state sovereignty, led the Court to conclude that it would be anomalous to allow such cases to be brought instead in state court.

In *Federal Maritime Comm'n v. South Carolina State Ports Authority*, the Court addressed the issue of whether state sovereign immunity extended to proceedings before federal agencies.[132] In this case, the South Carolina State Ports Authority denied a cruise ship permission to berth at the state's port facilities in Charleston, South Carolina, contending that the primary purpose of the cruise was for gambling. The cruise ship company, Maritime Services, filed a claim with the Federal Maritime Commission (FMC) arguing that South Carolina had discriminated against it in violation of the Shipping Act of 1984 and sought, among other things, damages for loss of profits.[133] The Port Authority, however, successfully moved to dismiss the complaint, arguing that it was inconsistent with the concept of state sovereign immunity.

In reviewing the case, the Court analogized between the FMC's quasi-judicial proceedings and traditional judicial proceedings, while noting that "[t]he preeminent purpose of state sovereign immunity is to accord States the dignity that is consistent with their status as sovereign entities."[134] Consequently, the Court agreed that state sovereign immunity bars the FMC from adjudicating damage claims made by a private party against a nonconsenting State.[135] In dissent, however, Justice Breyer noted that agency administrative proceedings are not judicial proceedings and that the ultimate enforcement of such proceedings in a court is done by the federal agency, to which state sovereign immunity does not apply. Thus, while an agency remains capable of enforcement actions against states in federal court, it cannot use its own adjudicative process to determine whether to do so, but must rely on its investigatory powers.[136] According to Justice Breyer, "[t]he natural result is less agency flexibility, a larger federal bureaucracy, less fair procedure, and potentially less effective law enforcement."[137]

The Spending Clause

It should be noted that in many instances, the federal government still has the ability to influence state behavior despite the constitutional limits discussed above.[138] One of the more significant ways that the federal government can encourage state behavior is to impose conditions on the receipt of federal monies by the states. Considering the large amount of funds provided to states by the federal government, this represents a significant power for Congress to exercise. Further, as the concept of grant conditioning can involve waiver by the states of Tenth and Eleventh Amendment rights, these grant conditions may allow Congress to indirectly achieve compliance by a state in a way that could not be achieved directly.

The question of whether a state can be required to perform (or refrain from) certain actions was addressed in the Supreme Court case of *South Dakota v. Dole*.[139] In *Dole*, Congress enacted the National Minimum Drinking Age Amendment of 1984,[140] which directed the Secretary of Transportation to withhold a percentage of federal highway funds from states in which the age for purchase of alcohol was below 21 years. The State of South Dakota, which permitted 19-yearolds to purchase beer, brought suit arguing that the law was an invalid exercise of Congress's power under the Spending Clause to provide for the "general welfare."[141] The Supreme Court held that, as the indirect imposition of such a standard was directed toward the general welfare of the country, it was a valid exercise of Congress's spending power.

The Court noted that the grant condition did not implicate an independent constitutional bar (i.e., the grant condition did not require the state to engage in an unconstitutional activity). Further, the court noted that the grant condition was not a violation of the Tenth Amendment, which generally prevents Congress from "commandeering" state legislatures[142] and executive branch officials[143] to implement federal programs.[144] The Tenth Amendment would not apply here, the Court held, because the state officials were voluntarily cooperating in order to receive federal grants, and thus were not being directed to comply with federal mandates.

The Court did suggest, however, that there were limits to Congress's power under the Spending Clause to require states to meet certain grant conditions. First, a grant condition must be related to the particular national projects or programs to which the money was being directed.[145] In *Dole*, the congressional condition imposing a specific drinking age was found to be related to the national concern of safe interstate travel, which was one of the main purposes for highway funds being expended. Second, the Court suggested that, in some circumstances, the financial inducements offered by Congress might be so coercive as to pass the point at which "pressure turns into compulsion."[146] In *Dole*, however, the percentage of highway funds that were to be withheld from a state with a drinking age below 21 was relatively small, so that Congress's program did not coerce the states to enact higher minimum drinking ages than they would otherwise choose.

One of the more controversial potential applications of this doctrine arises when the government requires that, in order to receive a grant, a state waive its sovereign immunity to suits brought by private citizens. As discussed above, the Supreme Court has imposed significant limits on Congress's ability to abrogate state sovereign immunity. However, this does not appear to have prevented the lower courts from finding that states can be required to waive their sovereign immunity as a condition of receiving grants.

A state's sovereign immunity, is "a personal privilege which it may waive at its pleasure."[147] Thus, it is clearly possible for a state, under some circumstances, to waive sovereign immunity as a condition of receiving federal funds.[148] The Supreme Court has held that "mere receipt of federal funds" is insufficient to constitute a waiver of state sovereign immunity.[149] However, the Court has also held that where a federal statute contains an "unambiguous waiver" of a state's

Eleventh Amendment immunity, then a state's acceptance of such funds can be an effective waiver.[150]

Thus, it would appear that the waiver of sovereign immunity as a grant condition would pass constitutional muster under *Dole.* Just as states may waive their Tenth Amendment rights not to be commandeered when accepting grant conditions (as noted in *Dole*), it seems generally accepted that there is no constitutional bar to a state voluntarily waiving its sovereign immunity rights.[151] As a general matter, conditioning a federal grant on the voluntary waiver of state sovereign immunity does not seem to be of particular constitutional concern.

Under *Dole*, however, a court would, on a case-by-case basis, need to examine the level of financial burden that would be imposed on the state by the withdrawal of a particular federal grant to ensure that the condition was not coercive. Further, under *Dole*, a court would need to examine how related the purpose of the proposed bill was to the waiver of sovereign immunity in connection with a particular grant program.[152] However, the Court in *Dole* indicated that it would show significant deference to Congress in determining whether a grant condition relates to an underlying federal program, and this requirement does not appear to have been of concern to lower courts considering waiver of sovereign immunity as a grant condition.[153]

CONCLUSION

It would appear that the status of the state in the federal system has been strengthened by recent Supreme Court opinions. Although the Court has not scaled back the federal government's substantive jurisdiction significantly, it has to some extent prevented the expansion of Congress's power under the Commerce Clause and under § 5 of the Fourteenth Amendment. Further it has created a variety of obstacles as to how these powers can be executed, forbidding Congress under the Tenth Amendment from commandeering the authority of state legislative and executive branches, and limiting the authority of Congress to abrogate state sovereign immunity. Ultimately, however, Congress retains significant powers to influence state behavior, such as through the Spending Clause, and, under the Supremacy Clause, Congress may require the enforcement of its laws in both state and federal court.

End Notes

[1] Portions of this report were prepared by Kristin Thornblad, legal intern.

[2] *See, e.g.*, U.S. Const. Art. I, § 10, cl. 2 ("No State shall ... lay any Imposts or Duties on Imports or Exports.")

[3] "No State shall, without the Consent of Congress, lay any Duty of Tonnage, keep Troops, or Ships of War in time of Peace, enter into any Agreement or Compact with another State, or with a foreign Power, or engage in War, unless actually invaded, or in such imminent Danger as will not admit of delay." U.S. Const., Art. I, § 10, cl. 3.

[4] "Full Faith and Credit shall be given in each State to the public Acts, Records, and Judicial Proceedings of every other State. And the Congress may by general Laws prescribe the Manner in which such Acts, Records, and Proceedings shall be proved, and the Effect thereof." U.S. Const. Art. IV, § 1. This "Full Faith and Credit Clause" gives Congress what amounts to enforcement authority over the required recognition by each state of the judgments, records, and legislation of other states.

[5] "... [N]o new State shall be formed or erected within the Jurisdiction of any other State; nor any State be formed by the Junction of two or more States, or parts of States, without the Consent of the Legislatures of the States concerned as well as of the Congress." U.S. Const., Art. IV, § 3, cl. 1.

[6] Gibbons v. Ogden, 22 U.S. (9 Wheat.) 1 (1824).

[7] Article I, § 1, of the Constitution provides that "All legislative powers herein granted shall be vested in a Congress of the United States." Unlike a typical grant of power to states Article I, § 1, does not grant to Congress "all legislative power," but rather grants to Congress only those specific powers enumerated in § 8 and elsewhere in the Constitution.

[8] As stated by Chief Justice Marshall in McCulloch v. Maryland, 17 U.S. (4 Wheat.) 316 (1819): "Let the end be legitimate, let it be within the scope of the Constitution, and all means which are appropriate, which are plainly adapted to that end, which are not prohibited, but consist with the letter and spirit of the Constitution, are constitutional."

[9] "The Congress shall have Power To lay and collect Taxes, Duties, Imposts and Excises, to pay the Debts and provide for the common Defence and general Welfare of the United States; but all Duties, Imposts and Excises shall be uniform throughout the United States." U.S. Const., Art. I, § 8, cl. 1.

[10] "No Money shall be drawn from the Treasury, but in Consequence of Appropriations made by Law." U.S. Const., Art. I, § 9, cl. 7.

[11] United States v. Butler, 297 U.S. 1 (1936).

[12] "To regulate commerce with foreign Nations, and among the several States, and with the Indian Tribes." U.S. Const., Article I, § 8, cl. 3.

[13] U.S. Const., Art. I, § 8, cl. 4.

[14] U.S. Const., Art. I, § 8 cl. 5.

[15] U.S. Const., Art. I, § 8, cl. 6.

[16] U.S. Const., Art. I, § 8, cl. 7.

[17] U.S. Const., Art. I, § 8, cl. 8.

[18] "The Congress shall have power ... To establish an uniform Rule of Naturalization." U.S. Const., Art I, § 8, cl. 4. "All persons born or naturalized in the United States and subject to the jurisdiction thereof are citizens of the United States and of the State wherein they reside." U.S. Const., Amend. XIV, § 1.

[19] "No State shall make or enforce any law which shall abridge the privileges or immunities of citizens of the United States; nor shall any State deprive any person of life, liberty, or property, without due process of law; nor deny to any person within its jurisdiction the equal protection of the laws." U.S. Const., Amend. XIV, § 1. The Congress shall have power to enforce, by appropriate legislation, the provisions of this article. *Id.* at § 5.

[20] U.S. Const., Amend. XXVI.

[21] U.S. Const., Amend. XV.

[22] U.S. Const., Amend. XIX.

[23] "The Times, Places and Manner of holding Elections for Senators and Representatives, shall be prescribed in each State by the Legislature thereof; but the Congress may at any time by Law make or alter such Regulations, except as to the Places of chusing Senators." U.S. Const., Article I, § 4, cl. 1. While the Fifteenth Amendment and the other voting rights guarantees noted above protect only against state action, congressional authority under this clause includes protection of the electoral process against private interference. A variety of enactments can be traced to this authority, including campaign finance laws and the Hatch Act (insofar as it applies to federal elections).

[24] "Each House shall be the Judge of the Elections, Returns and Qualifications of its own Members." Article I, § 5, cl. 1. The House and the Senate act as judicial tribunals in resolving contested election cases.

[25] *See, e.g.*, U.S. Const., Amend. XIV, § 2 (apportionment).

[26] "The Congress shall have power ... To exercise exclusive Legislation in all Cases whatsoever, over such District ... as may, by Cession of Particular States, and the Acceptance of Congress, become the Seat of the Government of the United States, and to exercise like Authority over all Places purchased by the Consent of the Legislature of the State in which the Same shall be, for the Erection of Forts, Magazines, Arsenals, dock-Yards and other needful Buildings." Article I, § 8, cl. 17. "The Congress shall have power to dispose of and make all needful Rules and Regulations respecting the Territory or other Property belonging to the United States...." Article IV, § 3, cl. 2.

[27] "[N]or shall private property be taken for public use, without just compensation." U.S. Const., Amend. V. Implicit in the Fifth Amendment's requirement that just compensation be paid for private property that is taken for a public use is the existence of the government's power to take private property for public use.

[28] *See, e.g.*, U.S. Const. Art. I, § 8, cl. 10 ("The Congress shall have power ... To define and punish Piracies and Felonies committed on the high Seas, and Offences against the Law of Nations"); U.S. Const., Art. I, § 8, cl. 11 ("... To declare War, grant Letters of Marque and Reprisal, and make Rules concerning Captures on Land and Water."); U.S. Const., Art. I, § 8, cl. 12 ("To raise and support Armies....").

[29] U.S. Const., Art. I, § 8, cl. 3.

[30] 514 U.S. 549 (1995).

[31] 18 U.S.C. § 922(q)(1)A).

[32] Abel, The Commerce Clause in the Constitutional Convention and in Contemporary Comment, 25 Minn. L. Rev. 432, 443-44 (1941); Greenspan, The Constitutional Exercise of the Federal Police Power: A Functional Approach to Federalism, 41 Vanderbilt Law Review 1019, 1022-24 (1988). Those materials which do address congressional control over commerce focus on the necessity of uniformity in matters of foreign commerce, although the drafters clearly intended domestic commerce to be regulated as well. P. Kurland & R. Lerner, THE FOUNDER'S CONSTITUTION 477-528 (1987).

[33] Alexander Hamilton, CONTINENTALIST, No. 5, 18 April 1782 (Paper 3:75-82) as reprinted in P. Kurland & R. Lerner, *supra* note 32 ("The vesting of the power of regulating trade ought to have been a principal object of the confederation for a variety of reasons. It is as necessary for the purposes of commerce as of revenue.")

[34] Greenspan, *supra* note 32 at 1023.

[35] Gibbons v. Odgen, 22 U.S. (9 Wheat.) 1, 197-98 (1824).

[36] *See, e.g.,* Brown v. Maryland, 25 U.S. (12 Wheat.) 419 (1827).

[37] United States v. Lopez, 514 U.S. at 593 (Thomas, J., dissenting).

[38] Champion v. Ames (The Lottery Case), 188 U.S. 321 (1903).

[39] Hippolite Egg Co. v. United States, 220 U.S. 45 (1911).

[40] Hoke v. United States, 227 U.S. 308 (1913).

[41] United States v. E.C. Knight Co., 156 U.S. 1, 12 (1895).

[42] Carter v. Carter Coal Co., 298 U.S. 238, 304 (1936).

[43] 301 U.S. 1 (1937).

[44] 301 U.S. at 41.

[45] United States v. Darby, 312 U.S. 100 (1941)(approving legislation relating to working conditions).

[46] 312 U.S. at 121.

[47] Wickard v. Filburn, 317 U.S. 111 (1942).

[48] *Id.*

[49] *See* Heart of Atlanta Motel v. United States, 370 U.S. 241 (1964); Katzenbach v. McClung, 379 U.S. 241 (1964).

[50] Perez v. United States, 402 U.S. 146 (1971).

[51] Herman Schwartz, *Court Tries to Patrol a Political Line,* Legal Times 25 (May 8, 1995).

[52] The Court failed to note that to some extent, the three categories are intertwined. For instance, the first category, the regulation of "streams" or "channels" of commerce, allows regulation of the creation, movement, sale and consumption of merchandise or services. But the initial extension of the "streams" of commerce analysis by the Court to intrastate trade was justified by the "effect" of these other activities on commerce. *See* NLRB v. Jones & Laughlin, 301 U.S. 1, 31 (1936). Similarly, the second category, which allows the regulation of such instrumentalities of commerce as planes, trains or trucks, is also based on the theory that a threat to these instrumentalities "affects" commerce, even if the effect is local in nature. Southern Railway Company v. United States, 222 U.S. 21, 26-27 (1911)(regulation of intrastate rail traffic has a substantial effect on interstate rail traffic). Thus, the final category identified by the Court appears to be a catch-all for all other activities which "substantially affect" commerce.

[53] 514 U.S. at 559.

[54] Wickard v. Filburn, 317 U.S. 111 (1942).

[55] 514 U.S. at 564. The Court rejected arguments that possession of guns in school affected the national economy by its negative impact on education. *Id.*

[56] 514 U.S. at 561.

[57] 514 U.S. at 560.

[58] 514 U.S. at 580 (Kennedy, J., concurring). The Court has reiterated its concern over extending Commerce Clause powers to Congress in areas of the law traditionally reserved to the states. *See, e.g.,* Solid Waste Agency of Northern Cook County (SWANCC) v. U.S. Army Corps of Engineers, 531 U.S. 159, 174 (2001) (rejecting an interpretation of the Clean Water Act which allowed regulation of nonnavigable, isolated wetlands as infringing upon the "traditional and primary state power over land and water use").

[59] *See, e.g.*, 18 U.S.C. § 247 (2000)(forbidding obstruction of persons in the free exercise of religious beliefs where the offense "is in or affects interstate or foreign commerce.")

[60] 529 U.S. 598 (2000).

[61] *Id.* at 609.

[62] The requirement that a commerce clause regulation be economic or commercial has been influential in a number of subsequent statutory interpretation cases. In Jones v. United States, 529 U.S. 848 (2000), a criminal defendant challenged his conviction under 18 U.S.C. § 844(i), which, in part, makes it a crime to destroy by fire or explosive a building "used" in interstate commerce. Applying the statutory canon that one should interpret a statute to avoid constitutional doubt, Jones v. United States, 526 U.S. 227, 239 (1999), the Court held that the statute did not apply to a private residence that was "used" as collateral to obtain and secure a loan, "used" to obtain insurance, and "used" to receive natural gas from other sources. The Court construed the statute to require that a building protected by § 844(i) be "actively employed" for commercial purposes, *id.* at 855, arguing that a broader interpretation would extend the statute to virtually every arson in the country. A similar result occurred in the case of Solid Waste Agency of Northern Cook County (SWANCC) v. U.S. Army Corps of Engineers, 531 U.S. 159 (2001). In *SWANCC*, the Court considered a challenge to the Migratory Bird Rule, 51 Fed. Reg. 41217, which extended § 404(a) of the Clean Water Act (CWA), 33 U.S.C. § 1344(a) to nonnavigable, isolated wetlands. The Court held that this interpretation of the statute would raise serious constitutional questions, requiring, for instance, a close examination of precisely what activity was being regulated. Absent a clear statement from Congress that it intended the Clean Water Act to

have such a broad reach, the Court found the rule was not supported by the statute. *Id.* at 173. *See also* Rapanos v. United States Army Corps of Engineers, 165 L. Ed. 2d 159, 201 (2006).

[63] 545 U.S. 1 (2005).

[64] Cal. Health & Safety Code Ann § 11362.5 (West Supp. 2005) (providing for the legal possession of medical marijuana by a patient or primary caregiver, upon the written or oral recommendation of a physician).

[65] 545 U.S. at 28.

[66] 317 U.S. 111 (1942).

[67] *Id.* at 125.

[68] 52 Stat. 31.

[69] *Id.* at 128-29.

[70] *Id.* at 127.

[71] 545 U.S. at 19.

[72] *Id.*

[73] U.S. Const., Art. I, § 8, cl. 18.

[74] 545 U.S. at 22.

[75] (Scalia, J., concurring) (citations omitted).

[76] Art. I, § 8, cl. 1 provides that "The Congress shall have Power to lay and collect Taxes, Duties, Imposts and Excises, to pay the Debts and provide for the common Defence and general Welfare of the United States; but all Duties, Imposts and Excises shall be uniform throughout the United States."

[77] 541 U.S. 600 (2004).

[78] 541 U.S. at 606.

[79] No. 08–1224 slip. op. (May 17, 2010).

[80] *Id.* at 22.

[81] 4 Wheat. 316, 421 (1819).

[82] U.S. Const., Amend. XIII (prohibiting slavery).

[83] U.S. Const., Amend. XV (voting rights).

[84] 384 U.S. 641 (1966).

[85] 400 U.S. 112 (1970).

[86] 521 U.S. 507 (1997).

[87] 494 U.S. 872 (1990).

[88] See notes 90-104 and accompanying text, *infra.*

[89] Seminole Tribe of Florida v. Florida, 517 U.S. 44, 65-66 (1996); *See* discussion *infra* notes 95-98 and accompanying text.

[90] 527 U.S. 666 (1999).

[91] 15 U.S.C. § 1125(a).

[92] 527 U.S. 627 (1999).

[93] Patent and Plant Variety Protection Remedy Clarification Act (Patent Remedy Act), 35 U.S.C. §§ 271(a).

[94] U.S. Const. Art. I, § 8, cl. 8.

[95] U.S. Const. Art. I, § 8, cl. 3.

[96] 528 U.S. 62 (2000).

[97] 531 U.S. 356 (2001).

[98] Cleburne v. Cleburne Living Center, Inc., 473 U.S. 432 (1985).

[99] 538 U.S. 721 (2003).

[100] 29 U.S.C. § 2612(a)(1)(C).

[101] 529 U.S. 598 (2000).

[102] *See supra* notes 60-61 and accompanying text.

[103] *See* Shelley v. Kraemer, 334 U.S. 1, 13 (1948).

[104] 521 U.S. at 526.

[105] 529 U.S. at 626.

[106] 541 U.S. 509 (2004).

[107] One plaintiff in *Lane* claimed he was unable to appear to answer criminal charges on the second floor of a courthouse that had no elevator. The second plaintiff, a certified court reporter, claimed she was denied the opportunity both to work and to participate in the judicial process because she was unable to access numerous county courthouses.

[108] The Court cited congressional evidence that legislative attempts preceding Title II inadequately addressed the problem of patterned unconstitutional treatment in access to the courts. 541 U.S. at 526.

[109] The Court held that it need not examine Title II as a whole when evaluating the remedy's congruence and proportionality to the injury of disability discrimination in access to the courts. The relevant inquiry solely concerned Title II's scope as applied to the rights associated with access to judicial services. The Court cited as precedent for this limited application approach the *Garrett* case, in which it considered only Title I of the ADA for purposes of Fourteenth Amendment analysis. Based on this narrow scope of inquiry, the Court determined that both the pattern of past discrimination in access to the courts and the failure of previous legislative attempts to remedy the injury were sufficient to hold that Title II is a valid exercise of Congress's power under § 5 of the Fourteenth Amendment.

[110] 541 U.S. at 529. As noted by Chief Justice Rehnquist in dissent, 541 U.S. at 541-42 (Rehnquist, C.J., dissenting), the congruence and proportionality analysis in the majority opinion in *Lane* did not limit itself to historical examples of the disabled being denied due process, but also cited a history of disparate treatment in other less protected areas. *See id*. at 524-25.

[111] Title II does not require states to compromise the integrity of public programs or make unduly burdensome changes to public facilities. 541 U.S. at 532. Rather, states need only take reasonable measures to comply with Title II regulations. *Id.*

[112] 125 S. Ct. 877 (2006).

[113] *Id.* at 881.

[114] 426 U.S. 833 (1976).

[115] In *National League of Cities v. Usery*, the Court conceded that the legislation under attack, which regulated the wages and hours of certain state and local governmental employees, was undoubtedly within the scope of the Commerce Clause, but it cautioned that there are attributes of sovereignty attaching to every state government which may not be impaired by Congress, not because Congress may lack an affirmative grant of legislative authority to reach the matter, but because the Constitution prohibits it from exercising the authority in that manner.

[116] 469 U.S. 528 (1985). Justice Blackmun's opinion for the Court in *Garcia* concluded that the *National League of Cities* test for "integral operations" in areas of traditional governmental functions had proven impractical, and that the Court in 1976 had "tried to repair what did not need repair."

[117] See also South Carolina v. Baker, 485 U.S. 505 (1988).

[118] 505 U.S. 144 (1992).

[119] 521 U.S. 898 (1997).

[120] "The Constitution and the Laws of the United States ... shall be the Supreme Law of the Land; and the Judges in every State shall be bound thereby...." U.S. Const., Art. VI, cl. 2.

[121] 528 U.S. 141 (2000).

[122] It should be noted that not all suits in which a state is involved is a "suit" against a state. In Tennessee Student Assistance Corp. v. Hood, 541 U.S. 440 (2004), the Court addressed state sovereign immunity in the context of bankruptcy proceedings. In that case, the Court addressed whether Eleventh Amendment immunity extended to an adversary proceeding initiated by a debtor seeking an undue hardship discharge of her state-held student loan debt. The Court held that the proceeding did not constitute a suit against the state for purposes of the Eleventh Amendment. The Court noted that the bankruptcy petition in question was an *in rem* proceeding, so that the court's jurisdiction was over the petitioner's debt, rather than over her person or the state. *Id.* at 448. Thus, the federal bankruptcy court's exercise of jurisdiction over the state-held debt did not infringe upon the state's sovereignty immunity. *Id.* at 450.

[123] 2 U.S. (Dall.) 419 (1793).

[124] U.S. Const., Art. III, § 2.

[125] 134 U.S. 1 (1890).
[126] *See* Alden v. Maine, 527 U.S. 706, 2248 (1999).
[127] 517 U.S. 44 (1996).
[128] U.S. Const., Art. I, § 8, cl. 3.
[129] 491 U.S. 1 (1989).
[130] One apparent argument is that the Fourteenth Amendment was passed after the Eleventh Amendment and thus, unlike legislative powers found in Article I of the Constitution, it can be seen as an alteration of the restrictions of the Eleventh Amendment. Seminole Tribe of Florida v. Florida, 517 U.S. 44, 65-66 (1996). However, as is discussed in detail below, the Supreme Court has held that state sovereign immunity preceded and predated the Constitution. Alden v. Maine, 527 U.S. 706, 2248 (1999). Consequently, all the Articles of the Constitution could arguably be seen as altering the restrictions of the state sovereign immunity. Another argument made by the Court in *Seminole* is that the Fourteenth Amendment was designed to alter the preexisting balance between state and federal power at the time of its passage. This argument is more plausible, but is still difficult to differentiate between Congress's power under the Fourteenth Amendment and Congress's power under the Articles of the Constitution. Like the Fourteenth Amendment, the Articles of the Constitution were clearly intended to alter the balance between state and federal power at the time of the passage of the Constitution, which included state sovereign immunity. This is exemplified by the Supremacy Clause, U.S. Const., Art. VI, cl. 2 which provides that laws passed under the Articles of the Constitution would be supreme over state law.
[131] 527 U.S. 706 (1999).
[132] 122 S. Ct. 186 (2002).
[133] 46 U.S.C. App. § 1701 (1994 & Supp. V).
[134] 122 S. Ct. at 1874.
[135] The Court noted that "[there are] numerous common features shared by administrative adjudications and judicial proceedings." 122 S. Ct. at 1872. "[F]ederal administrative law requires that agency adjudication contain many of the same safeguards as are available in the judicial process. The proceedings are adversary in nature. They are conducted before a trier of fact insulated from political influence. A party is entitled to present his case by oral or documentary evidence, and the transcript of testimony and exhibits together with the pleadings constitutes the exclusive record for decision. The parties are entitled to know the findings and conclusions on all of the issues of fact, law, or discretion presented on the record." *Id.*
[136] Justice Breyer noted that after this decision "a private person cannot bring a complaint against a State to a federal administrative agency where the agency (1) will use an internal adjudication process to decide if the complaint is well founded, and (2) if so, proceed to court to enforce the law." *Id.* at 1881.
[137] Id.
[138] For instance, the federal government has, in some cases, made the application of federal regulatory authority contingent, so that if a state chooses to regulate in that field, the federal regulatory role is circumscribed. In many cases, this will encourage states to regulate, so that the state has closer control of the application of such regulation within the state. *See, e.g.*, 42 U.S.C. § 7410 (national air control standards not applicable upon the adoption by states of adequate air control standards).
[139] 483 U.S. 203 (1987).
[140] 23 U.S.C. § 158.
[141] U.S. Const., Art I, 8, cl 1 (Congress has the power to "lay and collect Taxes, Duties, Imposts, and Excises, to pay the Debts and provide for the common Defence and general Welfare of the United States").
[142] New York v. United States, 505 U.S. 144 (1992).
[143] Printz v. United States, 521 U.S. 898 (1997).
[144] It would seem that sovereign immunity is a core state power, and that requiring its waiver would raise Tenth Amendment concerns. *See, e.g.*, National League of Cities v. Usery, 426 U.S. 833 (1976)(striking down federal wage and price controls on state employees as involving the regulation

of traditional state functions). As discussed previously, however, the Court has, for the time being, abandoned this line of cases. Garcia v. San Antonio Metropolitan Transit Authority, 469 U.S. 528 (1985)(concluding that the test to identify traditional governmental functions had proven impractical, and that such disputes should be resolved through the political process).

[145] 483 U.S. at 207.

[146] *Id.* at 211.

[147] College Savings Bank v. Florida Prepaid Postsecondary Education Expense Board, 527 U.S. 666, 674 (1999) *citing* Clark v. Barnard, 108 U.S. 436, 447 (1883).

[148] Since such a waiver must be voluntary, the Court will consider carefully whether a state has actually waived its immunity. Atascadero State Hospital v. Scanlon, 473 U.S. 234, 241 (1985). For instance, a court will generally only find a waiver to federal suit based on a state statute if a state makes a "clear declaration" that it intends to submit itself to federal jurisdiction. Great Northern Life Ins. Co. v. Read, 322 U.S. 47, 54 (1944). *See also* Pennhurst State School and Hospital v. Halderman, 465 U.S 89, 99 (1984) (State's consent to suit must be "unequivocally expressed").

[149] Atascadero State Hospital v. Scanlon, 473 U.S. 234 (1985). In *Atascadero State Hospital,* the Court held that if a statute "manifests a clear intent to condition participation in the programs funded under the Act on a State's waiver of its constitutional immunity," federal courts would have jurisdiction over claims against states accepting federal funds. *Id.* at 247.

[150] Lane v. Pena, 518 U.S. 187, 200 (1996). For instance, Section 504 of the Rehabilitation Act of 1973, 29 U.S.C. § 701, *et seq.* provides that "a state shall not be immune under the Eleventh Amendment of the Constitution of the United States from suit in Federal court for a violation of section 504 of the Rehabilitation Act of 1973...." 42 U.S.C. § 2000d-7(a)(1). Consequently, a number of United States Courts of Appeals have found that receipt of federal funding subject to this condition was sufficient to waive a state's sovereign immunity. Koslow v. Commonwealth of Pennsylvania Department of Corrections; 302 F.3d 161 (3rd Cir. 2002); Nihiser v. Ohio EPA, 269 F.3d 626 (6th Cir. 2001); Jim C. v. United States, 235 F.3d 1079 (8th Cir. 2000); Stanley v. Litscher, 213 F.3d 340, 344 (7th Cir. 2000); Pederson v. La. St. Univ., 213 F.3d 858, 875-76 (5th Cir. 2000); Sandoval v. Hagan, 197 F.3d 484, 493-94 (11th Cir. 1999), rev'd on other grounds, 532 U.S. 275 (2001); Litman v. George Mason Univ., 186 F.3d 544, 554 (4th Cir. 1999); Clark v. California, 123 F.3d 1267, 1271 (9th Cir. 1997).

[151] Susan M. Luken, Irreconcilable Differences: the Spending Clause and the Eleventh Amendment: Limiting Congress's Use of Conditional Spending to Circumvent Eleventh Amendment Immunity,70 U. Cin. L. Rev. 693 (2002); Michael T. Gibson, Congressional Authority to Induce Waivers of State Sovereign Immunity: The Conditional Spending Power (and Beyond), 29 Hastings Const. L.Q. 439 (2002); Litman v. George Mason University. 186 F.3d 544 (4th Cir. 1999); Jim C. v. United States, 235 F.3d 1079 (8th Cir. 2000).

[152] *See id.* at 1084 (Bowman, J., dissenting) (arguing that waiver of sovereign immunity was not related to purpose of education grants).

[153] *See generally* Litman v. George Mason University, 186 F.3d 544 (4th Cir. 1999); Jim C. v. United States, 235 F.3d 1079 (8th Cir. 2000).

The Basis and Limitations of Congressional… ISBN: 978-1-61324-160-8
Editors: A. P. Boehm, M. D. Angello

Chapter 2

THE POWER TO REGULATE COMMERCE: LIMITS ON CONGRESSIONAL POWER*

Kenneth R. Thomas[1] and Todd B. Tatelman[2]

SUMMARY

The Commerce Clause of the United States Constitution provides that the Congress shall have the power to regulate interstate and foreign commerce. The plain meaning of this language might indicate a limited power to regulate commercial trade between persons in one state and persons outside of that state. However, the Commerce Clause has never been construed quite so narrowly. Rather, the clause, along with the economy of the United States, has grown and become more complex. In addition, when Congress began to address national social problems, the Commerce Clause was often cited as the constitutional basis for such legislation. As a result, the Commerce Clause has become the constitutional basis for a significant portion of the laws passed by the Congress over the last fifty years, and it currently represents one of the broadest bases for the exercise of congressional powers. The reliance of the Congress on the Commerce Clause, however, has been controversial, as was the case with the passage of the Patient Protection and Affordable Care Act (PPACA, P.L. 111-148).

An examination of the United States Code shows that over 700 statutory provisions, covering a range of issues, explicitly refer to either

---

* This is an edited, reformatted and augmented version of a Congressional Research Services publication, dated December 28, 2010.

"interstate" or "foreign" commerce. Over the last decade, however, the Supreme Court in *United States v. Lopez* and *United States v. Morrison* has brought into question the breadth of the Commerce Clause. While these cases have resulted in the overturning of a few federal laws, their overall effect has so far been relatively modest in scope. A recently decided Supreme Court case, *Gonzales v. Raich*, seems to confirm that the effect of these previous cases will be limited.

BACKGROUND

The Commerce Clause (Art. I, § 8, cl. 3) of the United States Constitution provides that the Congress shall have the power to regulate interstate and foreign commerce. The plain meaning of this language might indicate a limited power to regulate commercial trade between persons in one state and persons outside of that state. However, the Commerce Clause has never been construed quite so narrowly. Rather, the clause, along with the economy of the United States, has grown and become more complex. In addition, when Congress began to address national social problems, the Commerce Clause was often cited as the constitutional basis for such legislation. As a result, the Commerce Clause has become the constitutional basis for a significant portion of the laws passed by the Congress over the last fifty years, and it currently represents one of the broadest bases for the exercise of congressional powers. The reliance of Congress on the Commerce Clause, however, has been controversial, as was the case with the passage of the Patient Protection and Affordable Care Act (PPACA).[1]

An examination of the United States Code shows that more than 700 statutory provisions explicitly refer to either "interstate" or "foreign" commerce, covering a significant number of issues. These issues include agriculture,[2] banking,[3] antitrust,[4] securities,[5] business regulation,[6] energy regulation,[7] hazardous substances,[8] consumer credit,[9] sports regulation,[10] the internet,[11] endangered species,[12] civil rights,[13] child support,[14] child pornography,[15] abortion,[16] criminal law,[17] controlled substances,[18] food,[19] firearms control,[20] terrorism,[21] obscenity,[22] gambling devices,[23] labor,[24] industrial safety,[25] pensions,[26] environmental law,[27] fish and wildlife,[28] medical products,[29] water pollution,[30] atomic energy,[31] shipping,[32] motor vehicle safety,[33] airplanes,[34] and tort litigation.[35]

Recent Supreme Court case law, however, has brought the limits of the Commerce Clause into question.[36] While these cases have resulted in the overturning of federal laws, their overall affect has so far been relatively modest in scope. A recently decided Supreme Court case, *Gonzales v. Raich*,[37] seems to confirm that the effect of these previous cases will be limited.

Textual Analysis

The Commerce Clause provides that "The Congress shall have Power .. To regulate Commerce with foreign Nations, and among the several States and with the Indian Tribes." The word "commerce" appears to have the same primary meaning today as it did in 1789—"an interchange of goods or commodities between different countries or between areas of the same country" or in other words "trade."[38] However, commentators have argued that a secondary meaning of commerce which was understood at the time of the drafting of the Constitution includes all productive activity which relates to commerce, such as manufacturing and agriculture.[39]

A further question is then raised whether Congress's power to regulate commerce is significantly limited by the phrase "with foreign Nations, and among the several states, and with the Indian Tribes." For instance, the phrase "among the several States" could either be interpreted as "between people of different states" or more broadly as "between people who live in the various states." Some have argued that the broader definition, which would cover commerce between people of the same state, would render the phrase "among the several States" superfluous.[40] This question, generally characterized as whether the power to regulate "interstate commerce" extends to "intrastate" commerce has been mostly settled by case law, and most "intrastate" commercial transactions are vulnerable to some form of federal regulation.[41]

Drafting and Ratification

The integration of commercial activities in the United States was a central theme of the Constitutional Convention of 1787.[42] It appears, however, that the parameters of the Commerce Clause were not of particular concern to the framers of the Constitution.[43] The commentary contemporary to the Constitution on the power did not concern itself with the federalism implications of managing interstate economic transactions, but rather focused on the issue of foreign trade.[44] The primary purpose of the clause appears to have been raising federal revenue by the nationalization of the states' power to impose import tariffs,[45] while a secondary purpose was apparently to allow

Congress to regulate and restrict foreign commerce to advance American interests.[46]

The argument has been made that while regulating free and fair trade between states was the principal motivation for adopting various other provisions of the Constitution,[47] it may not have been a strong motivation for the drafting of the Commerce Clause. This is because state restrictions on trade between states were already prohibited under the Articles of Confederation, and the states generally complied with these restrictions.[48] Consequently, commentary contemporary to the ratification of the Constitution indicating that the Commerce Clause was intended to limit state restrictions on interstate commerce was minimal.

Case Law Development

In *Gibbons v. Ogden,* the Supreme Court, in an opinion by Chief Justice Marshall, considered a challenge to a monopoly on the operation of steam-propelled vessels in New York waters. This monopoly was challenged by Gibbons, who transported passengers from New Jersey to New York under an act of Congress. The Chief Justice, in striking down the monopoly, wrote that "the power over commerce ... is vested in Congress as absolutely as it would be in a single government ..." and that "the influence which their constituents possess at elections, are ... the sole restraints" on this power.[49]

The Chief Justice went on to write that "[t]he counsel for the appellee would limit [the term commerce] to traffic, to buying and selling, or the interchange of commodities, and do not admit that it comprehends navigation. This would restrict a general term, applicable to many objects, to one of its significations. Commerce, undoubtedly, is traffic, but it is something more—it is intercourse," which the Court found easily included the issue of navigation. Marshall did qualify the word "intercourse" with the word "commercial," thus retaining the element of monetary transactions.

The Court did not soon revisit this expansive view of the Commerce Clause. Instead, over the next several decades, the Court considered the boundaries of the "dormant Commerce Clause" doctrine—the implied limitation of the Commerce Clause on a state's ability to regulate commerce.[50] This, combined with the relatively cautious exercise of the power by the early Congresses, meant that the Supreme Court did not have occasion to consider the limits of the Congress's power under this doctrine for almost sixty years.

When the Court again revisited Congress's power under the clause, it generally approved of statutes regulating the interstate movement of goods or persons, such as lottery tickets,[51] adulterated food,[52] or prostitutes.[53] But, during the early 1900s, the Supreme Court was confronted with statutes which went beyond regulation of trade, and addressed other related economic activities. Consequently, the Court struck down a series of federal statutes which attempted to extend commerce regulation to activities such as "production," "manufacturing"[54] or "mining."[55]

Starting in 1937, however, with the decision in *NLRB v. Jones & Laughlin Steel Corporation*,[56] the Supreme Court held that Congress has the ability to protect interstate commerce from burdens and obstructions which "affect" commercial transactions. In the *NLRB* case, the court upheld the National Labor Relations Act, finding that by controlling industrial labor strife, Congress was preventing burdens from being placed on interstate commerce.[57] Thus, the Court rejected previous distinctions between the economic activities (such as manufacturing) which led up to interstate economic transactions, and the interstate transactions themselves. By allowing Congress to regulate activities which were in the "stream" of commerce, the Court also set the stage for the regulation of a variety of other activities which "affect" commerce.

Subsequent Court decisions found that Congress had considerable discretion in regulating activities which "affect" interstate commerce, as long as the legislation was "reasonably" related to achieving its goals of regulating interstate commerce.[58] Thus the Court found that in some cases, events of purely local commerce (such as local working conditions) might, because of market forces, negatively affect interstate commerce, and thus would be susceptible to regulation.[59] The Court has also held that an activity which in itself does not affect interstate commerce could be regulated if all such activities taken together in the aggregate did affect interstate commerce.[60] Under the reasoning of these cases, the Court has upheld many diverse laws, including laws regulating production of wheat on farms,[61] racial discrimination by businesses,[62] and loan-sharking.[63]

In the 1995 case of *United States v. Lopez,*[64] however, the Supreme Court brought into question the extent to which the Congress can rely on the Commerce Clause as a basis for federal jurisdiction. Under the Gun-Free School Zone Act of 1990, Congress made it a federal offense for "any individual knowingly to possess a firearm at a place that the individual knows, or has reasonable cause to believe, is a school zone."[65] In *Lopez*, the Court held that, because the act neither regulated a commercial activity nor contained a requirement that the possession was connected to interstate commerce, the act exceeded the authority of Congress under the Commerce Clause. Although the Court did not explicitly overrule any previous rulings upholding federal statutes passed under the authority of the Commerce Clause, the decision would appear to suggest new limits to Congress's legislative authority.

The *Lopez* case was significant in that it was the first time since 1937 that the Supreme Court struck down a federal statute purely based on a finding that the Congress had exceeded it powers under the Commerce Clause.[66] In doing so, the Court revisited its prior cases, sorted the commerce power into three categories, and asserted that Congress could not go beyond these three categories: 1) regulation of channels of commerce; 2) regulation of instrumentalities of commerce; and 3) regulation of economic activities which "affect" commerce.[67]

Within the third category of activities which "affect commerce," the Court determined that the power to regulate commerce applies to intrastate activities only when they "substantially" affect commerce.[68] Still, the Court in *Lopez* spoke approvingly of earlier cases upholding laws which regulated intrastate credit transactions, restaurants utilizing interstate supplies, and hotels catering to interstate guests. The Court also recognized that while some intrastate activities may by themselves have a trivial effect on commerce, regulation of these activities may be constitutional if their regulation is an essential part of a larger economic regulatory scheme. Thus, the Court even approved what has been perceived as one of its most expansive rulings, *Wickard v. Filburn*, which allowed the regulation of the production of wheat for home consumption.[69]

The Court in *Lopez* found, however, that the Gun Free School Zones Act fell into none of the three categories set out above. It held that it was not a regulation of channels of commerce, nor did it protect an instrumentality of commerce. Finally, its effect on interstate commerce was found to be too removed to be "substantial." The Court noted that the activity regulated, the possession of a gun in a school zone, neither by itself nor in the aggregate affected commercial transactions.[70] Further, the statute contained no requirement that interstate commerce be affected, such as that the gun had been previously transported in interstate commerce.[71] Nor was the criminalization of possession of a gun near a school part of a larger regulatory scheme which did regulate commerce.[72] Finally, the Court indicated that criminal law enforcement is an area of law traditionally reserved to the states.[73] Consequently, the Court found that Congress did not have the authority to pass the Gun Free School Zone Act.

The Court also discussed the absence of legislative findings with respect to the statute's effect on interstate commerce.[74] While noting that Congress is not formally required to make such findings, the Court nevertheless held that "to the extent that congressional findings would enable us to evaluate the legislative judgment that the activity in question substantially affected interstate commerce, even though no such substantial effect was visible to the naked eye, they are lacking here."[75]

Although the Supreme Court has confirmed the dictates of *Lopez* in the case of *United States v. Morrison*,[76] discussed *infra*, both of these decisions dealt primarily with the issue of "substantial impact" on commerce. However, as noted, the Court has identified two other categories of power that Congress has under the Commerce Clause—regulation of channels of commerce and regulation of instrumentalities of commerce—that have been interpreted almost as broadly. Thus, an evaluation of the impact of these cases requires an examination of all three categories of power.

THE THREE CATEGORIES OF COMMERCE CLAUSE JURISPRUDENCE

Channels of Commerce

The channels of commerce doctrine has been interpreted so as to represent a broad power to regulate. To begin with, this category is the basis for a variety of statutes that directly regulate the movement of persons or goods across state lines. For instance, the United States Code contains extensive references to mailing or shipping material in interstate commerce, including regulations or bans on shipping biological agents,[77] counterfeit documents,[78] explosives,[79] or threatening communications.[80]

Of more significance is that the Court has not required that any nexus exist between the time that a person crosses a state border and the time they engage in a prohibited activity. For instance, in *United States v. Sullivan*,[81] the Court addressed the application of § 301k of the Federal Food, Drug and Cosmetic Act to a local pharmacist. The section prohibits the "doing of any ... act with respect to, a ... drug ... if such act is done while such article is held for sale after shipment in interstate commerce and results in such article being misbranded." The pharmacist was charged with "misbranding" sulfathiazole by not providing sufficient information regarding dosage and usage.

The Court in *Sullivan* relied on previous precedent finding that Congress has not only the power regulate commerce among the states, but also the power to "keep the channels of such commerce free from the transportation of illicit or harmful articles."[82] The fact that the defendant here had bought the item after it had passed over state lines was not found to be of constitutional significance.[83] Thus, the Court appears to require only that the criminal activity in question has some relation to the crossing of state lines.

Consistent with this line of reasoning, there are laws, such as criminal prohibitions on mail fraud,[84] where the material is regulated not because it is by nature harmful, but rather because it relates to other behavior which is criminal. Or, there are laws prohibiting crimes based on a person crossing the state line with the intent to commit the sexual abuse of minors, where it is the activity engaged in after the line is crossed that is criminal.[85] Finally, there are laws that regulate activities which utilize materials after they have been shipped in interstate commerce, even if the materials were perfectly legal when they were transported.[86]

Ultimately, based on cases such as *Sullivan*, it would appear that statutes that would otherwise be in violation of the limitations of *Lopez* could be approved by courts because of the presence of the jurisdictional element that an item related to the crime had crossed a state line. Under this reasoning, the gun possession law struck down in *Lopez,* which has since been amended to require that the gun had previously been shipped in interstate commerce,[87] would be upheld.[88] Thus, an expansive reading of the channels of commerce doctrine would appear to stand in the way of a limited interpretation of the Commerce Clause.

Instrumentalities of Interstate Commerce

Under the "instrumentalities of commerce" category, Congress may properly make whatever regulations it sees fit for the safety, efficiency, and accessibility of the nationwide transportation and communications networks. For instance, in *Preseault v. I.C.C.*,[89] the Court considered whether Congress could prevent the reversion of railroad rights-of-way to property owners after abandonment in order to create recreational trails. The I.C.C. argued that turning the right-of-ways into recreation trails was preserving the rail corridors for future railroad use. Despite arguments that the preservation argument was a pretext, the Court held that it must defer to a congressional finding that a regulated activity affects interstate commerce "if there is any rational basis for such a finding."[90]

The instrumentalities of commerce category represents yet another significant basis for expansive congressional authority. As noted previously, federal mail and wire fraud statutes make it a crime to engage in fraud while using the telephone or the mails. By analogy, Congress could reach many other activities that utilize these networks or similar networks such as railroads, interstate highways, and even the Internet. While this category has not been fully occupied by Congress, it would appear that a significant amount of federal power could be exercised in this manner, regardless of whether the matter regulated involved non-economic activity.[91] The Court has not yet indicated whether the *Lopez* requirement that regulated activities have some connection to a commercial activity would be applicable in this category.

Substantial Impact on Interstate Commerce

Wickard v. Filburn

The third prong of Congress's power to regulate under the Commerce Clause involves those activities that have a substantial impact or effect on interstate commerce. To fully understand the scope and reach of this power, it is important to begin with an examination of the Court's 1942 decision in *Wickard v. Filburn*,[92] which led to the expansive view of the Commerce Clause that Congress operated under until 1995. In *Wickard*, the Court was asked to determine whether, under the Commerce Clause, amendments to the Agricultural Adjustment Act of 1938 implementing a quota system to restrict the amount of wheat that could be harvested and sold, applied to individuals who produced and consumed homegrown bushels of wheat.[93]

In upholding the statute as constitutional, the Court held that economic activities, regardless of their nature, could be regulated by Congress if the activity "asserts a substantial impact on interstate commerce...."[94] The Court reasoned that the growing of wheat, even if only for a family's personal consumption, provided an alternative to the marketplace that was both viable and competitive.[95] Although the Court admitted that one family's production alone would likely have a negligible impact on the overall price of wheat, if combined with other personal producers the effect would be substantial enough to make the activity subject to congressional regulation.[96] The rationale of combining individual effects to find substantial impacts on interstate commerce has become known as the "aggregation theory," and arguably represents the most far reaching example of Congress's authority to regulate under the Commerce Clause.[97]

Lopez and Morrison

After *Wickard*, the Court consistently held that a "rational basis" existed for Congress to enact laws under the theory that the regulated behavior substantially affected interstate commerce.[98] Despite the consistency of these decisions, it was not always clear whether the activity in question met the "substantially affects" test. Then in 1995, when the Court decided the *Lopez* case, as discussed previously, it explored the limits of the "substantially affects" test.

Subsequently, in *United States v. Morrison*,[99] the Court invalidated a portion of the Violence Against Women Act, which specifically created a private right of action against anyone who committed such a crime, allowing an injured party to obtain damages and other compensatory relief.[100] Applying its holding in *Lopez*, the Court concluded that the activity regulated by the act could not be classified as "economic activity," and therefore the aggregation principle established by *Wickard* did not apply. The Court, however, stopped short of establishing a rule that all noneconomic activity cannot be aggregated.[101] In addition, the Court concluded that the act contained no jurisdictional element connecting the creation of a federal cause of action for gender-motivated violence to Congress's power to regulate interstate commerce.[102]

Further, while in *Morrison*, unlike in *Lopez*, there were numerous congressional findings, the Court stressed that although findings by the legislative branch can serve to illuminate the relationship between the regulation and interstate commerce, constitutionality ultimately turns on the legal aspects of the substantial effects doctrine, and therefore, is for the Court to decide.[103] In this case, the Court found that the legislative findings detailing the effects on interstate commerce by gender motivated violence were based in large part on the "costs of crime," which was nearly identical to the reasoning expressly rejected by the Court in *Lopez*.[104]

Finally, the Court considered the level of attenuation between the regulated activity and its effect on interstate commerce. In this case, the Court concluded that the regulation of gender-motivated violent crime was not directed at the instrumentalities, channels or goods involved in interstate commerce, and was therefore beyond the scope of Congress's authority.[105]

In sum, after *Lopez* and *Morrison*, the test to determine whether a regulation has a substantial effect on interstate commerce requires reviewing courts to consider the following four factors: (1) whether the regulated activity is commercial or economic in nature; (2) whether an express jurisdictional element is provided in the statute to limit its reach; (3) whether Congress made express findings about the effects of the proscribed activity on interstate commerce; and (4) whether the link between the prohibited activity and the effect on interstate commerce is attenuated.[106]

Gonzales v. Raich

After the decision in *Lopez* and *Morrison,* the question arose as to whether these cases were a harbinger of future restrictions on Congress's power to legislate. Arguably, the Court had intended *Lopez* and *Morrison* to have a limited effect, as the Court specifically reaffirmed much of its previous Commerce Clause case law. Further, the statutory provisions challenged in *Lopez* (criminal penalties for gun possession in or near schools) and *Morrison* (civil suits for gender-motivated crime) were relatively unusual for statutes based on the commerce clause in that they did not contain a specific requirement that the activities be related to commerce. In addition, while broad economic regulation may have noneconomic elements (e.g., record-keeping requirements), the provisions in question were activities were not associated with such larger schemes.

Accordingly, when provisions contained in broader regulatory schemes were challenged after *Lopez* and *Morrison,* the lower courts generally upheld these under a "broader scheme" doctrine.[107] This doctrine is largely derived from language in *Lopez* that arguably permits congressional regulation of noneconomic activity if the regulation is "an essential part of a larger regulatory scheme, in which the regulatory scheme would be undercut unless the intrastate activity was regulated."[108]

Nonetheless, it was suggested by some commentators that certain non-economic provisions of larger regulatory schemes might also be successfully challenged. These challenges were generally characterized as "as applied" challenges. Generally, a court reviewing the constitutionality of a federal statute may declare the statute unconstitutional either as invalid on its face,[109] or "as applied" to a particular set of circumstances.[110] Utilizing an "as applied" standard, various lower courts struck down particular applications of broader statutory schemes.[111]

When presented with an "as applied" challenge, these courts initially attempted to define the relevant "class of activity" presented by the facts of the specific case. For instance, in the Ninth Circuit case of *Ashcroft v. Raich*, the court considered a challenge to the Controlled Substances Act. The challenging parties were seriously ill California residents who had obtained marijuana consistent with California's Compassionate Use Act[112] but in violation of the federal Controlled Substances Act (CSA).[113] The Ninth Circuit found the class of activity to be the "intrastate, noncommercial cultivation, possession and use of marijuana for personal medical purposes on the advice of a physician and in accordance with state law."[114] Having defined the relevant class of activity, the court proceeded to apply the four factor *Morrison* test.

With respect to the first factor—whether or not the activity is commercial or economic in nature—the court concluded that the narrow class of activity in this case could not be considered commercial or economic in nature.[115] The court next considered whether the CSA contains an express jurisdictional element that would limit its reach to those cases that substantially affect interstate commerce. With no stated analysis, and apparently persuaded by the reasoning of a district court opinion, the court concluded that "[n]o such jurisdictional hook exists in the relevant portions of the CSA."[116]

With respect to whether the legislative history contains congressional findings regarding the effects on interstate commerce, the court was able to cite findings relating to the effect that intrastate drug trafficking activity would have on interstate commerce.[117] While admitting that the legislative history lends support to the constitutionality of the statute under the Commerce Clause, the court proceeded to diminish the importance of these findings by arguing that they were not specific to either marijuana or the medicinal use of marijuana, but rather related to the general effects of drug trafficking on interstate commerce.[118] In addition, the court referred to language in *Morrison*, discussing the limited role of congressional findings.[119] Moreover, the court referenced Ninth Circuit precedent concluding that the first and fourth prongs of the *Morrison* test—whether the statute regulates an economic enterprise and whether the link is attenuated—are the most significant factors to the analysis.[120]

Finally, with respect to whether the link between the regulated activity and a substantial effect on interstate commerce is attenuated, the court expressed doubt that the interstate effect of homegrown medical marijuana is substantial. Citing authority questioning the validity of the federal government's claim of an effect on interstate commerce,[121] the court concluded that "this factor favors a finding that the CSA cannot constitutionally be applied to the class of activities at issue in this case."[122]

The United States Supreme Court granted *certiorari* specifically on the question of whether the power vested in Congress by both the "Necessary and Proper Clause," and the "Commerce Clause" of Article I includes the power to prohibit the local growth, possession, and use of marijuana permissible as a result of California's law.[123] Justice Stevens, writing for the majority in the now-entitled *Gonzales v. Raich*, reversed the Ninth Circuit's decision and held that Congress's power to regulate commerce extends to purely local activities that are "part of an economic class of activities that have a substantial effect on interstate commerce."[124]

In reaching its conclusions, the Court relied heavily on its 1942 decision in *Wickard v. Filburn*, which held that the Agricultural Adjustment Act's federal quota system applied to bushels of wheat that were homegrown and personally consumed. *Wickard* stands for the proposition that Congress can rationally combine the effects that individual producers have on a commercial market to find substantial impacts on interstate commerce.[125] The Court pointed to numerous similarities between the facts presented in *Raich* and those in *Wickard*. Initially, the Court noted that because the commodities being cultivated in both cases are fungible and that well-established interstate markets exist, both markets are susceptible to fluctuations in supply and demand based on production intended for home-consumption being introduced into the national market.[126]

According to the Court, just as there was no difference between the wheat Mr. Wickard produced for personal consumption and the wheat cultivated for sale on the open market, there is no discernable difference between personal home-grown medicinal marijuana and marijuana grown for the express purpose of being sold in the interstate market.[127] Thus, the Court concluded that Congress had a rational basis for concluding that "leaving home-consumed marijuana outside federal control would similarly affect price and market conditions."[128]

Respondents argued that *Wickard* was distinguishable because in the case of wheat the activity involved was purely commercial, and the evidence clearly established that the aggregate production of wheat had a significant effect on the interstate market. Conversely, respondents claimed that the activity at issue in *Raich* is non-commercial—the respondents had never attempted to sell their marijuana—and Congress had made no finding that the personal cultivation and use of medicinal marijuana has a substantial effect on the interstate marijuana market.[129] The Court, however, noted that the standard for assessing the scope of Congress's power under the Commerce Clause, is not whether the activity at issue, when aggregated, substantially affects interstate commerce; but rather, whether there exists a "rational basis" for Congress to have concluded as such.[130] The Court, applying this deferential standard, concluded that "Congress had a rational basis for believing that failure to regulate the intrastate manufacture and possession of marijuana would leave a gaping hole in the CSA."[131] Moreover, the Court affirmed that

"Congress was acting well within its authority to 'make all Laws which shall be necessary and proper' to 'regulate Commerce among the several States.'"[132]

Despite having concluded that under the "rational basis test" Congress had acted within its constitutional authority when it enacted the CSA and applied it to intrastate possession of marijuana, the Court nevertheless had to distinguish *Lopez* and *Morrison*, the Court's more recent Commerce Clause decisions. The Court concluded that the CSA, unlike the statutes in either *Lopez* (Gun Free School Zones Act) or *Morrison* (Violence Against Women Act), regulated activity that is "quintessentially economic," therefore, neither *Lopez* or *Morrison* cast any doubts on the constitutionality of the statute.[133] The Court specifically rejected the reasoning used by the Ninth Circuit, concluding that "Congress acted rationally in determining that none of the characteristics making up the purported class, whether viewed individually or in the aggregate, compelled an exemption from the CSA; rather, the subdivided class of activities defined by the Court of Appeals was an essential part of the larger regulatory scheme."[134]

In supporting its conclusions, the Court noted that, by characterizing marijuana as a "Schedule I" narcotic, Congress was implicitly finding that it had no medicinal value at all. In addition, the Court returned to the fact that medicinal marijuana was a fungible good, thus making it indistinguishable from the recreational versions that Congress had clearly intended to regulate. According to the Court, to carve out medicinal use as a distinct class of activity, as the Ninth Circuit had done, would effectively make "*any* federal regulation (including quality, prescription, or quantity controls) of *any* locally cultivated and possessed controlled substance for *any* purpose beyond the 'outer limits' of Congress'[s] Commerce Clause authority."[135] Moreover, the Court held that California's state law permitting the use of marijuana for medicinal purposes cannot be the basis for placing the respondent's class of activity beyond the reach of the federal government, due to the Supremacy Clause, which requires that, in the event of a conflict between state and federal law, the federal law shall prevail.[136]

Finally, the Court responded to the respondent's argument that its activities are not an "essential part of a larger regulatory scheme" because they are both isolated and policed by the State of California and they are completely separate and distinct from the interstate market.[137] The Court held that not only could Congress have rationally rejected this argument, but also that it "seem[ed] obvious" that doctors, patients, and caregivers will increase the supply and demand for the substance on the open market.[138] In sum, the Court concluded that the case for exemption can be distilled down to an argument that a locally grown product used domestically is immune from federal regulation, which has already been precluded by the Court's decision in *Wickard v. Filburn.*[139]

End Notes

[1] P.L. 111-148. See CRS Report R40725, Requiring Individuals to Obtain Health Insurance: A Constitutional Analysis, by Jennifer Staman et al.

[2] See, e.g., 7 U.S.C. § 6a (2005)(prohibition on excessive commodity speculation); 7 U.S.C. § 6b (2005)(prohibition on fraud, false reporting, or deception in commodities).

[3] See, e.g., 12 U.S.C. § 95 (2005)(regulation of the banking business; powers and duties of national banks); 12 U.S.C. § 2501 (2005)(disposition of abandoned money orders and traveler's checks).

[4] See, e.g., 15 U.S.C. § 26b (2005) (application of the antitrust laws to professional major league baseball).

[5] See, e.g., 15 U.S.C. § 77e (2005)(domestic securities; prohibitions relating to interstate commerce and the mails); 15 U.S.C. § 77l (2005)(civil liabilities arising in connection with prospectuses and communications.

[6] 15 U.S.C. § 79h (2005)(public utility holding companies; acquiring interest in electric and gas companies serving same territory); 15 U.S.C. § 79i (2005)(public utility holding companies; acquisition of securities and utility assets and other interests).

[7] See, e.g., §15 U.S.C. § 715b (2005)(interstate transportation of petroleum products; interstate transportation of contraband oil forbidden);15 U.S.C. § 717 (2005)(natural gas; regulation of natural gas companies); 16 U.S.C. § 813 (power entering into interstate commerce; regulation of rates, charges).

[8] See, e.g., 15 U.S.C. § 1263 (2005)(hazardous substances; prohibited acts); 15 U.S.C. § 1265 (2005)(hazardous substances; seizures); 15 U.S.C. § 1270 (2005)(hazardous substances; examinations and investigations); 15 U.S.C. § 1271 (2005)(hazardous substances; records of interstate shipment).

[9] See, e.g., 15 U.S.C. § 1644 (2005)(consumer credit protection; fraudulent use of credit cards; penalties); 15 U.S.C. § 1679a (2005)(consumer credit protection; credit repair organizations).

[10] See, e.g., 15 U.S.C. § 6307b (2005)(professional boxing safety; protection from coercive contracts).

[11] See, e.g., 15 U.S.C. § 7704 (2005)(non-solicited pornography and marketing; protections for users of commercial electronic mail).

[12] 16 U.S.C. § 1538 (2005)(endangered species; prohibited acts).

[13] See, e.g., 18 U.S.C. § 245 (2005)(civil rights; federally protected activities); 42 U.S.C. § 2000a (2005)(civil rights; prohibition against discrimination or segregation in places of public accommodation).

[14] 18 U.S.C. § 228 (failure to pay legal child support obligations).

[15] 18 U.S.C. § 2251 (sexual exploitation of children).

[16] 18 U.S.C. § 1531 (partial-birth abortions prohibited).

[17] There are over a hundred criminal laws which use the term "interstate commerce." See, e.g., 18 U.S.C. § 1033 (2005)(fraud and false statements; crimes by or affecting persons engaged in the business of insurance whose activities affect interstate commerce); 18 U.S.C.§ 33 (destruction of motor vehicles or motor vehicle facilities); 18 U.S.C. § 1952 (interstate and foreign travel or transportation in aid of racketeering enterprises); 18 U.S.C. § 1958 (use of interstate commerce facilities in the commission of murder-for-hire).

[18] See, e.g., 21 U.S.C. § 801 (2005)(drug abuse prevention and control; congressional findings and declarations); 21 U.S.C. § 863 (2005)(drug abuse prevention and control; drug paraphernalia).

[19] See, e.g., 21 U.S.C. § 602 (meat inspection; congressional statement of findings).

[20] See, e.g., 26 U.S.C. § 5861 (2005)(machine guns, destructive devices, and certain other firearms; prohibited acts).

[21] See, e.g.,18 U.S.C. § 2332a (use of weapons of mass destruction).

[22] 18 U.S.C. § 1462 (importation or transportation of obscene matter).

[23] See, e.g., 15 U.S.C. § 1172 (2005)(transportation of gambling devices as unlawful; exceptions; authority of Federal Trade Commission).

[24] See, e.g., 29 U.S.C. § 207 (2005)(fair labor standards; maximum hours).

[25] See, e.g., 29 U.S.C. § 651 (2005)(occupational safety and health; congressional statement of findings and declaration of purpose and policy).

[26] See, e.g., 29 U.S.C. § 1001 (2005)(employee retirement income security program; congressional findings); 29 U.S.C. § 1001a (2005)(employee retirement income security program; additional findings).

[27] See, e.g., 33 U.S.C. § 1322 (2005)(water pollution prevention and control; marine sanitation devices); 42 U.S.C. § 7671d (2005)(stratospheric ozone protection; phase-out of production and consumption of class II substances).

[28] 16 U.S.C. § 3372 (2005)(fish and wildlife; prohibited acts).

[29] See, e.g., 42 U.S.C. § 262 (2005)(licensing of biological products and clinical laboratories; regulation of biological products).

[30] See, e.g., 42 U.S.C. § 300j-23 (2005)(safety of public water systems; drinking water coolers containing lead).

[31] See, e.g., 42 U.S.C. § 2012 (2005)(atomic energy; findings); 42 U.S.C. § 2019 (2005)(atomic energy: applicability of federal power act); 42 U.S.C. § 2073 (2005)(special nuclear material; domestic distribution of special nuclear material).

[32] See, e.g., 46 U.S.C. § 4307 (2005)(recreational vessels; prohibited acts); 46 U.S.C. § 4311 (2005)(recreational vessels; penalties and injunctions); 46 U.S.C. appendix § 801 (2005)(shipping act; definitions).

[33] See, e.g., 49 U.S.C. § 30101 (2005)(motor vehicle safety; purpose and policy); 49 U.S.C. § 30112 (2005)(motor vehicle safety; prohibitions on manufacturing, selling, and importing noncomplying motor vehicles and equipment); 49 U.S.C. § 30123 (2005)(motor vehicle safety; tires).

[34] See, e.g., 49 U.S.C. § 40116 (2005)(air commerce and safety; state taxation).

[35] P.L. 109-2 (Class Action Fairness Act of 2005).

[36] United States v. Lopez, 514 U.S. 549, 561 (1995); United States v. Morrison, 529 U.S. 598 (2000).

[37] ___ U.S. ___, 125 S. Ct. 2195 (2005).

[38] Grant Nelson and Robert Pushaw, Jr., Rethinking the Commerce Clause: Applying First Principles to Uphold Federal Commercial Regulations but Preserve State Control Over Social Issues, 85 Iowa L. Rev. 1, 101 n 478 (2001). As will be discussed later, a requirement that the thing to be regulated be "commercial" or "mercantile," has, to some extent, been used by the Supreme Court to limit the commerce power to "commercial" activities. See United States v. Lopez, 514 U.S. 549, 561 (1995); United States v. Morrison, 529 U.S. 598, 617 (2000).

[39] Grant Nelson and Robert Pushaw, Jr., supra footnote 38, at 14-15.

[40] Randy Barnett, The Original Meaning of the Commerce Clause, 68 U. CHI. L. REV. 101, 132 (2001).

[41] See "Case Law Development," infra.

[42] Virginia and Maryland had just finished a compact regarding the navigation and jurisdiction of the Chesapeake Bay and the Potomac. The commissioners who had negotiated this treaty called for a general trade convention, and various other states responded by appointing delegates to this convention. Only when it became clear that this convention might address other issues did the Continental Congress approve of it. J. Story, Commentaries on the Constitution of the United States 252-54.

[43] Abel, The Commerce Clause in the Constitutional Convention and in Contemporary Comment, 25 MINN. L. REV.

432, 443-44 (1941); Greenspan, The Constitutional Exercise of the Federal Police Power: A Functional Approach to Federalism, 41 VANDERBILT LAW REVIEW 1019, 1022-24 (1988).

[44] Those materials which do address congressional control over commerce focus on the necessity of uniformity in matters of foreign commerce, although the drafters clearly intended domestic commerce to be regulated as well. P. Kurland & R. Lerner, THE FOUNDER'S CONSTITUTION 477-528 (1987).

[45] Alexander Hamilton, CONTINENTALIST, No. 5, 18 Apr. 1782 (Paper 3:75-82) as reprinted in P. Kurland & R. Lerner, supra footnote 44 ("The vesting of the power of regulating trade ought to have been a principal object of the confederation for a variety of reasons. It is as necessary for the purposes of commerce as of revenue.") For instance, the state of New York imposed a 2% impost on imports that moved through the New York Harbor. Calvin Johnson, The Panda's Thumb: The Modest and Mercantilist Original Meaning of the Commerce Clause, 13 WM. & MARY BILL OF RIGHTS JOURNAL 8 (2004). Efforts under the Articles of Confederation to impose a federal impost on imports had been blocked by New York. Id. at 11-12. Granting the Congress the power to raise revenue in this manner was seen as an important way to pay off Revolutionary War debts. Id. at 8-11.

[46] For instance, the prospect of excluding British ships from American waters, while never realized, was contemplated as a retaliation for the exclusion of American ships from the British West Indies. Calvin Johnson, supra footnote 45, at 35-36.

[47] Such provisions include the limitation on state duties and imposts on imports and exports, U.S. CONST. Article I, § 10, cl. 2, as such duties had favored states with deep harbors over neighbor states; the Port Preference Clause, U.S. CONST., Art. I, § 9, cl. 6, limiting the federal government from imposing preferences for the ports of one state over another; and the prohibition on states issuing paper money, U.S. CONST., Art. I, § 10, cl. 1, the issuance of which had allowed states to require the acceptance of devalued money by out-of-state creditors. Id. at 46-48.

[48] Id. at 42-42.

[49] Gibbons v. Odgen, 22 U.S. (9 Wheat.) 1, 197-98 (1824).

[50] For a discussion of this case law, see Martin Redish and Shane Nugent, The Dormant Commerce Clause and the Constitutional Balance of Federalism, 1987 DUKE L.J. 569 (1987).

[51] Champion v. Ames (The Lottery Case), 188 U.S. 321 (1903).

[52] Hippolite Egg Co. v. United States, 220 U.S. 45 (1911).

[53] Hoke v. United States, 227 U.S. 308 (1913).

[54] United States v. E.C. Knight Co., 156 U.S. 1, 12 (1895).

[55] Carter v. Carter Coal Co., 298 U.S. 238, 304 (1936).

[56] 301 U.S. 1 (1937).

[57] 301 U.S. at 41.

[58] United States v. Darby, 312 U.S. 100 (1941)(approving legislation relating to working conditions).

[59] 312 U.S. at 121.

[60] Wickard v. Filburn, 317 U.S. 111 (1942).

[61] Id.

[62] Heart of Atlanta Motel v. United States, 370 U.S. 241 (1964); Katzenbach v. McClung, 379 U.S. 241 (1964).

[63] Perez v. United States, 402 U.S. 146 (1971).

[64] 514 U.S. 549 (1995).

[65] 18 U.S.C. §922(q)(1)A).

[66] Herman Schwartz, Court Tries to Patrol a Political Line, Legal Times 25 (May 8, 1995).

[67] The Court failed to note that to some extent, the three categories are intertwined. For instance, the first category, the regulation of "streams" or "channels" of commerce, allows regulation of the creation, movement, sale and consumption of merchandise or services. But the initial extension of

the "streams" of commerce analysis by the Court to intrastate trade was justified by the "effect" of these other activities on commerce. See NLRB v. Jones & Laughlin, 301 U.S. 1, 31 (1936). Similarly, the second category, which allows the regulation of such instrumentalities of commerce as planes, trains or trucks, is also based on the theory that a threat to these instrumentalities "affects" commerce, even if the effect is local in nature. Southern Railway Company v. United States, 222 U.S. 21, 26-27 (1911)(regulation of intrastate rail traffic has a substantial effect on interstate rail traffic). Thus, the final category identified by the Court appears to be a catch-all for all other activities which "substantially affect" commerce.

68 514 U.S. at 559.

69 Wickard v. Filburn, 317 U.S. 111 (1942).

70 514 U.S. at 564. The Court rejected arguments that possession of guns in school zones affected the national economy by its negative impact on education. Id.

71 514 U.S. at 561.

72 514 U.S. at 560.

73 514 U.S. at 580 (Kennedy, J., concurring).

74 Id.

75 Id. at 563.

76 529 U.S. 598 (2000).

77 18 U.S.C. § 175b.

78 18 U.S.C. § 514.

79 18 U.S.C. § 842.

80 18 U.S.C. § 876.

81 332 U.S. 689 (1948).

82 McDermott v. Wisconsin, 228 U.S. 115, 128 (1913).

83 332 U.S. at 697-98.

84 18 U.S.C. § 1341.

85 18 U.S.C. § 2241.

86 18 U.S.C. § 2252(a)(4)(B)(distributing child pornography where materials used have traveled in interstate commerce).

87 18 U.S.C. § 922(q)(2)(see Historical Notes).

88 But see United States v. McCoy, 323 F.3d 1114, 1124- 1126 (9th Cir. 2003) (reversing a conviction for possession of child pornography where jurisdiction was based on movement of photographic materials over state lines).

89 494 U.S. 1 (1990).

90 494 U.S. at 17, citing Hodel v. Virginia Surface Mining & Reclamation Assn., Inc., 452 U.S. 264, 276 (1981).

91 See Jesse Choper, Taming Congress's Power Under the Commerce Clause: What Does the Near Future Portend, 55 ARK. L. REV. 731, 761-762 (2003).

92 Wickard v. Filburn, 317 U.S. 111, 113-114 (1942).

93 In 1941, Mr. Filburn harvested an excess amount of 239 bushels for which he was fined $117.11 pursuant to amendments to the Agricultural Adjustment Act of 1938. Id. at 114.

94 Id. at 125.

95 Id. at 128.

96 Id.

97 See United States v. Lopez, 514 U.S. 549, 560 (1995).

98 See, e.g., Hodel v. Virginia Surface Mining & Reclamation Assn., Inc., 452 U.S. 264, 276-280 (1981); Perez v. United States, 402 U.S. 146, 155-156 (1971); Katzenbach v. McClung, 379 U.S. 294, 299-301 (1964); Heart of Atlanta Motel, Inc. v. United States, 379 U.S. 241, 252-253 (1964).

99 United States v. Morrison, 529 U.S. 598 (2000).

[100] 42 U.S.C. § 13981 (2000). In Morrison, a female plaintiff brought suit under the act against two men who had allegedly assaulted and raped her. The plaintiff asserted that her right to be free from gender associated violence had been violated, and therefore, she was entitled to monetary damages. See Morrison, 529 U.S. at 599 (2000).

[101] Id. (stating that "while we need not adopt a categorical rule against aggregating the effects of any non-economic activity in order to decide these cases, thus far in our Nation's history our cases have upheld Commerce Clause regulation of interstate activity only where that activity is economic in nature.").

[102] Id. (holding that because of the lack of jurisdictional element, "Congress elected to cast § 13981's remedy over a wider, and more purely intrastate, body of violent crime").

[103] Id.

[104] Id. at 615 (stating that the reasoning of Congress would supply it with the power to "regulate any crime as long as the nationwide, aggregated impact of that crime has substantial effects on employment, production, transit or consumption.").

[105] Id. at 618 (holding that "the regulation and punishment of intrastate violence that is not directed at the instrumentalities, channels, or goods involved in interstate commerce has always been the province of the States.").

[106] United States v. Stewart, 348 F.3d 1132, 1136-37 (9th Cir. 2003)(citing Morrison, 529 U.S. at 610-12).

[107] For example, numerous federal circuit courts have upheld the constitutionality of federal child pornography statutes that criminalize intrastate possession by finding the activity sufficiently connected to Congress's broader scheme of regulating the interstate commercial market for child pornography. See, e.g., United States v. Adams, 343 F.3d 1024, 1034 (9th Cir. 2003); see also United States v. Hampton, 260 F.3d 832 (8th Cir. 2001); United States v. Corp, 236 F.3d 325 (6th Cir. 2001); United States v. Kallestad, 236 F.3d 225 (5th Cir. 2000); United States v. Angle, 234 F.3d 326 (7th Cir. 2000); United States v. Rodia, 194 F.3d 465 (3d Cir. 1999); United States v. Robinson, 137 F.3d 652 (1st Cir. 1998); United States v. Buculei, 262 F.3d 322 (4th Cir. 2001); United States v. Galo, 239 F.3d 572 (3d Cir. 2001); United States v. Bausch, 140 F.3d 739 (8th Cir. 1998); but see United States v. McCoy, 323 F.3d 1114 (9th Cir. 2003); United States v. Corp, 236 F.3d 325 (6th Cir. 2001).

[108] Lopez, 514 U.S. at 561.

[109] According to the Supreme Court, "[a] facial challenge to a legislative Act is, of course, the most difficult challenge to mount successfully, since the challenger must establish that no set of circumstances exists under which the Act would be valid." United States v. Salerno, 481 U.S. 739, 745 (1987) (holding that the Bail Reform Act of 1984 is not facially invalid) (emphasis added).

[110] An "as applied" challenge is less difficult to sustain than a facial challenge because the challenger has to establish only that the statute is invalid when applied to the specific set of factual circumstances presented. Thus, some scholars had posited that since Lopez and Morrison were decided, "as applied" challenges to federal statutes for violation of the Commerce Clause would be more successful than have facial challenges See Brannon P. Denning & Glenn H. Reynolds, Rulings and Resistance: The New Commerce Clause Jurisprudence Encounters the Lower Courts, 55 ARK. L. REV. 1253, 1262 (2003) [hereinafter Denning & Reynolds] (noting that a review of lower court decisions between 2000 and 2003 indicates that while only one statute has been found facially unconstitutional, there had been multiple decisions handed down holding that federal statutes are unconstitutional as applied to their specific facts).

[111] Raich v. Ashcroft, 352 F.3d 1222 (9th Cir. 2003), rev'd, sub nom. Gonzales v. Raich, ___ U.S. ___, 125 S.Ct. 2195 (2005)(holding that possession of marijuana for medicinal purposes consistent with California state law did not substantially impact commerce, and thus was outside of Congress' authority to regulate); United States v. Stewart, 348 F.3d 1132 (9th Cir. 2003) (reversing a possession of an illegal machine-gun conviction because the statute failed to satisfy

the Lopez/Morrison standard); United States v. McCoy, 323 F.3d 1114 (9th Cir. 2003) (reversing a conviction for possession of child pornography because the statute failed to provide the necessary relationship to interstate commerce to justify Congress's power); United States v. Lynch, 265 F.3d 758 (9th Cir. 2001) (vacating a Hobbs Act conviction and remanding to district court for determination of whether the robbery of an individual is within scope of statute); United States v. Odom, 252 F.3d 1289 (11th Cir. 2001) (reversing convictions under federal arson statute where subject of arson was a church); United States v. Johnson, 246 F.3d 749 (5th Cir. 2001) (refusing to reconsider prior decision vacating guilty plea of defendant for burning down one-story church building under federal arson statute); United States v. Peterson, 236 F.3d 848 (7th Cir. 2001) (granting reversal of Hobbs Act conviction because there was no evidence of connection with interstate commerce as required by the statute); United States v. Corp, 236 F.3d 325 (6th Cir. 2001) (reversing conviction under federal child pornography statute based on interstate movement of photographic materials where it was conceded that defendant kept pictures for personal use and did not intend to sell or trade pictures); United States v. Ryan, 227 F.3d 1058 (8th Cir. 2000) (reversing and remanding a conviction under federal arson statute for arson of vacant fitness center); United States v. Wang, 222 F.3d 234 (6th Cir. 2000) (reversing a Hobbs Act conviction and noting attenuated connection to interstate commerce where criminal act directed toward individual as opposed to business); United States v. Ramey, 217 F.3d 842 (4th Cir. 2000) (vacating sentence under federal arson statute in light of Jones v. United States, 529 U.S. 848 (2000)); United States v. Rayborn, 138 F. Supp. 2d 1029 (W.D. Tenn. 2001) (discussing motion to reconsider dismissal of indictment for arson and finding that the church was not actively used in interstate commerce and that none of its activities affects interstate commerce).

[112] Cal. Health & Safety Code § 11362.5 (1996) (allowing the use of marijuana for medical purposes upon the recommendation of a licensed physician).

[113] 21 U.S.C. § 841(a)(1) (2003) (classifying marijuana as a "Schedule I" controlled substance and as such making it illegal to "manufacture, distribute or dispense, or possess with the intent to manufacture, distribute, or dispense a controlled substance" unless provided for in the statute).

[114] Id. at 1229.

[115] Raich, 352 F.3d at 1230 (stating that the "cultivation, possession, and use of marijuana for medicinal purposes and not for exchange or distribution is not properly characterized as commercial or economic activity").

[116] Id. at 1231 (citing County of Santa Cruz v. Ashcroft, 279 F. Supp. 2d 1192, 1209 (N.D. Cal. 2003)).

[117] Id. at 1232 (citing 21 U.S.C. § 801, which states that "federal control of intrastate incidents of the traffic in controlled substances is essential to the effective control of the interstate incidents such as traffic.").

[118] Id. at 1232.

[119] Id. (citing Morrison, 529 U.S. at 614).

[120] Id. at 1232-33 (citing United States v. McCoy, 323 F.3d 1114, 1119 (9th Cir. 2003)).

[121] Id. at 1233 (quoting Conant v. Walters, 309 F.3d 629, 647 (9th Cir. 2002) (stating that "[m]edical marijuana, when grown locally for personal consumption, does not have any direct or obvious effect on interstate commerce. Federal efforts to regulate it considerably blur the distinction between what is national and what is local.") (Kozinski, J., concurring)).

[122] Id.

[123] Gonzales v. Raich, ___ U.S. ___, 125 S. Ct. 2195 (2005).

[124] Id. at 2205 (citing Perez v. United States, 402 U.S. 146, 151 (1970)). The final outcome was 6-3 with Justice Stevens writing for himself and Justices Souter, Kennedy, Breyer, and Ginsburg. Justice Scalia, via a separate opinion, concurred only in the Court's judgment. See id. at 2215. Justice O'Connor dissented and filed an opinion that both Chief Justice Rehnquist and Justice Thomas joined in part. See id. at 2221. In addition, Justice Thomas filed his own dissenting opinion. See id. at 2229.

[125] Wickard v. Filburn, 317 U.S. 111, 125 (1942) (holding that, economic activity, regardless of its nature, can be regulated by Congress if the activity "asserts a substantial impact on interstate commerce ...").

[126] Raich, 125 S.Ct. at 2207, n. 29. The Court noted that the while the marijuana market is an illegal or illicit market, this fact appears to be of no legal or constitutional significance as Congress's power arguably encompasses both lawful and unlawful interstate markets. See id. (citing Lopez, 514 U.S. at 571, (Kennedy, J., concurring) (stating that "[i]n the Lottery Case, 188 U.S. 321 (1903), the Court rejected the argument that Congress lacked [the] power to prohibit the interstate movement of lottery tickets because it had power only to regulate, not to prohibit.").

[127] Raich, 125 S.Ct. at 2207.

[128] Id. (stating that "we had no difficulty concluding that Congress had a rational basis for believing that, when viewed in the aggregate, leaving home-consumed wheat outside the regulatory scheme would have a substantial influence on price and market conditions. Here too, Congress had a rational basis for concluding that leaving home-consumed marijuana outside federal control would similarly affect price and market conditions.") (internal citations omitted).

[129] Id.

[130] Id. at 2208-09 (citing Lopez, 514 U.S. at 557; see also Hodel v. Virginia Surface Mining & Reclamation Assn., Inc., 452 U.S. 264, 276-280 (1981); Perez, 402 U.S. at 155-156).

[131] See Raich, 125 S.Ct. at 2209.

[132] Id.

[133] Id. at 2209-10.

[134] Id. at 2211.

[135] Id. at 2212 (emphasis in original).

[136] Id.

[137] Id. at 2213.

[138] Id. 2213-14 (stating that "[i]ndeed that the California exemptions will have a significant impact on both the supply and demand sides of the market for marijuana is not just 'plausible' as the principal dissent concedes, ... it is readily apparent").

[139] Id. at 2215.

CHAPTER SOURCES

Chapter 1 - This is an edited, reformatted and augmented version of a Congressional Research Services publication, RL30315, dated July 12, 2010.

Chapter 2 - This is an edited, reformatted and augmented version of a Congressional Research Services publication, RL32844, dated December 28, 2010.

INDEX

G

H

I

J

L

M